MARY DORMER HARRIS

The Life and Works of a Warwickshire Historian

MARY DORMER HARRIS AGED AROUND THIRTY.
Her first book on Coventry was published in 1898 when she was thirty-one.

MARY DORMER HARRIS

The Life and Works of a Warwickshire Historian

Best wishes,
Jean Field

Jean Field

BREWIN BOOKS

First published by Brewin Books Ltd
Studley, Warwickshire B80 7LG in 2002
www.brewinbooks.com

ISBN 1-85858-199-0 Hardback
ISBN 1-85858-198-2 Paperback

British Library Cataloguing in Publication Data
A Catalogue record for this book is available from the British Library.

Printed in Great Britain by
Alden Press, Osney Mead, Oxford, OX2 0EF

CONTENTS

TO MY HUSBAND STANLEY

THE FRONT COVER shows a photograph of Bond's Hospital and the Bablake School in Coventry, taken by the author in 2001.
THE BACK COVER shows Joan, daughter of Richard, Earl of Arundel. After the death of her first husband she married William Beauchamp, fourth son of Thomas Beauchamp, third Earl of Warwick of that name. William was created Lord Abergavenny in 1392 and died in 1411. Joan survived him by many years and died in 1435. Portraits of both Lord and Lady Abergavenny were amongst the illustrations in the last book transcribed and edited by Mary Dormer Harris "The Register of the Guild of the Holy Trinity (etc) of Coventry" as both were probably members of that Guild.

FOREWORD

Sadly I did not have the pleasure of meeting Mary Dormer Harris because she had died before I was appointed Coventry's first City Archivist in 1938. Yet within a short time she became one of my best friends because of her published work on the history of Coventry and Warwickshire.

As City Archivist my primary responsibility was to be in charge of Coventry's records preserved in the muniment room in St Mary's Hall which had been constructed in 1895. John Cordy Jeaffreson had sorted and arranged the collection of records at that time and a *Catalogue* was published in 1896. Frederick Smith, the Town Clerk, had produced a *Supplementary Catalogue* in 1931.

My task was to build on the work that had been done and to develop a City Records Office.

I found that under the general supervision of the Town Clerk individual researchers had been given permission to consult the records and that from the 1890's Mary Dormer Harris had devoted considerable time to exploring the collections for her book *Life in an old English Town* published in 1898. This was a masterly introduction to the early history of Coventry and its success led her to embark on a lifetime's study of the history of Coventry based on its records.

As described in this book her publications provide evidence of her unique knowledge of the original sources for her writings and of her ability to present her research in an interesting manner to the lay reader. Her outstanding achievements were the edited transcription of the *Coventry Leet Book* published in parts by the Early English Text Society between 1907 and 1913 and her contribution to the *Victoria County History of Warwickshire*.

Apart from Coventry Mary Dormer Harris had wide and varied interests in an amazing range of Warwickshire history, including her knowledge of Stratford-upon-Avon and Shakespeare. Reading her books I am sure she thoroughly enjoyed sharing her scholarship with others.

Had Mary Dormer Harris lived before Colville published his *Worthies of Warwickshire* in 1869 she would certainly have been one of the worthies he included. It is therefore a special pleasure for me to welcome and commend this commemorative volume.

I congratulate all concerned in its preparation and production.

LEVI FOX
COVENTRY CITY ARCHIVIST 1938 - 1945
DIRECTOR EMERITUS OF THE SHAKESPEARE BIRTHPLACE TRUST

PREFACE

Although she merited a short obituary in "The Times" on 6th March 1936 Mary Dormer Harris was not a well-known name except in her own academic and literary circles and in her native Warwickshire. Yet in the sixty-six years since her death many more people have come to know her name and to ponder on what sort of a person she was. Martyn Davies, a very helpful young friend who owns a secondhand and antiquarian bookshop in Leamington Spa, told me that he was often asked about Mary Dormer Harris by people who had come to know and love her various books about Coventry and Warwickshire. Thus I hope that this book will provide an increased interest in her works. It says much for her scholarship, charisma and character that after her sudden death in 1936, two posthumous volumes were published and a Memorial Bursary Fund was set up to help needy students about to embark on a course of higher education.

In the course of the sixty-four years since this fund was set up by public subscription, nearly one hundred young people have been helped. The fund is administered by a group of Trustees and I am proud to say that since 1998 I have been one of these Trustees.

It is far easier for us to comprehend history if we discover a personal link, and since Mary Dormer Harris lived close to my paternal grandparents and maternal great-grandparents in Leamington Spa for the last forty years of her life, I feel that I have a family link to her life and times. Ellen Box (née Needle) my paternal grandmother, and Mary Sharp (née Ledbrook) my maternal great-grandmother, were both born around the same year as Mary Dormer Harris; both just a few miles from her birthplace in Stoneleigh in mid-Warwickshire. Mary Sharp was generally known within the family as Polly, so it was no surprise to me to learn that Mary Dormer Harris was often known as Molly. At the end of their lives all three women were buried in the same cemetery in Leamington, not far apart; Mary Dormer Harris in 1936, Mary Sharp in 1947 and Ellen Box in 1949.

However, although she was very firmly a middle-class Warwickshire woman of her times, and born with advantages which Ellen Box and Mary Sharp never had, in many ways Mary Dormer Harris lived a sadder and more difficult life than either of them. Despite this, I have the feeling that no matter in what period she had been born, or what obstacles had presented themselves, she would have succeeded in life, for she was a highly talented individual with enormous drive and energy. She was on the cutting edge of the cause of feminism in this country and quietly and with little fuss, she made her brilliant way in a man's world, making it easier for ambitious females who followed.

In June 2001 I was fortunate enough to make contact with Nancy Dormer Gutch, a second cousin of Mary Dormer Harris, who lives in Warwickshire like so many of her ancestors. Miss Dormer Gutch has in her possession various family photographs, letters and cuttings and I am deeply grateful for her co-operation and permission to include extracts from these items. It was very satisfying for me to be able to visit a relation who recalled visiting Mary Dormer Harris in Leamington when a small child and I came to understand the vital importance of family visits in the preservation of oral history.

In the course of my research I have been helped by a number of groups and individuals. The current Trustees of the Mary Dormer Harris Memorial Bursary have been extremely supportive throughout, and without their collective help this book would not have been possible. I have particular reason to thank Chairman, Shirley Reading; Secretary, Graham Cooper; Treasurer, Syd Creed; Caroline Haynes, former Secretary; and Angela Cameron, former Chairman of the Bursary Trust. In 1992 Angela prepared a file full of cuttings and reminiscences concerning Mary Dormer Harris and this provided me with an invaluable, and easily-accessible, source of facts. Angela also made available various notes written by the late Gertrude Bark, who had hoped to write a biography of her friend, and from these I have gleaned several interesting anecdotes.

I would like to extend special thanks to Councillor David Chater, currently Lord Mayor of Coventry and Councillor William Gifford, currently Town Mayor of Leamington Spa; also Roger Vaughan, Arts and Heritage Officer in Coventry; plus the Chief Archivist and Staff of Coventry City Archives. From there I was able to obtain a number of photographs and particular thanks are due to Jane Pudsey, the conservator. The County Archivist and staff of Warwickshire County Record Office have, as ever, been very helpful; their photographer "Nick the Pics" and large photograph collection making my life much easier. Thanks are also due to the Archivist and Librarian of Lady Margaret Hall in Oxford and the Archivist and Staff of the Records Office, Shakespeare Birthplace Trust, Stratford upon Avon.

Dr Levi Fox, who has written a Foreword for this book, has been particularly helpful and I am greatly indebted to him.

I would also like to thank other officials of the Dugdale Society, the Secretary of the Society of Antiquaries of London, the Librarian and staff of Coventry Central Library, the staff of Birmingham City Archives, the staff of Oxford Local Studies Department at Oxford Central Library, the Librarian at Richmond and Twickenham Local Studies Centre, the archivist of the Oxford University Press, various staff of the Bodeleian Library, Oxford, the Local History Librarians of Camden, Holborn and Islington Libraries and Dorothy Fenner, David Ellis and other members of the Loft Theatre in Leamington Spa. The BBC Written Archives Centre in Reading and the Coventry Mummers' Group have supplied specialist material for which I am very grateful.

Individuals who deserve special mention are Carol Pratt (for information on

Suffragists), Kathleen Hanks of the Leamington Literary Society, Paul Morgan, Nigel Cameron, Phyllis Woodruff, Margaret Lang, Ena Burton, Joan Greenwood, Ian Box, Rhianna Chinn, Christine Short, Mrs I. Short of Coventry and the late Edna King of Bishop's Tachbrook.

Writer and lecturer Bill Gibbons has patiently answered numerous questions about Leamington, and historian and writer David McGrory of Coventry has not only lent a selection of photographs from his own collection, but has also given invaluable help in other ways, not least conducting me on several long tours of St Mary's Hall in Coventry.

I have done my best to contact and acknowledge copyright holders of both photographs and texts, but if I have failed to make contact with any individuals, I will endeavour to rectify ommissions in future editions.

Since Mary Dormer Harris was known to different people by different names, I have included a variety of references to her in this book. Sometimes it seemed appropriate to use her full name, but often I have abbreviated this to MDH, whilst at other times Molly and Dor creep in. This last name was given her by a small boy around 1929, who once shouted "Mummy, Dor's coming" as he spied her beloved dumpy figure approaching their house. So Dor she then became to many young friends.

I would like to end by quoting from Mary Dormer Harris's Preface to her book "Unknown Warwickshire", dated May 1924. She wrote, *"This book is no 'furniture for the scholar's library.'"*

I can only add that neither is my book, but if it causes others to look afresh at the writings of a truly great Warwickshire historian, then I shall be well-satisfied.

ACKNOWLEDGEMENTS FOR ILLUSTRATIONS

1) Frontispiece - Mary Dormer Harris *(By permission of Coventry City Council)*
2) Dale House, Kenilworth, 1979. *(Memorial Bursary Archives)*
3) James Dormer *(By courtesy of Miss Dormer Gutch)*
4) Dale House 1979, Trustees in garden. *(Memorial Bursary Achives)*
5) A childhood note by MDH. *(Memorial Bursary Archives)*
7) The Legend of Rostrappe. *(Memorial Bursary Archives)*
10) The buildings of Lady Margaret Hall, Oxford *(Reproduced with kind permission of the Governing Body of Lady Margaret Hall, Oxford)*
11) A close-up of Mary Dormer Harris from the 1886 group *(Reproduced with kind permission of the Governing Body of Lady Margaret Hall, Oxford)*
12) Florence Hayllar from a college group in 1887 *(Reproduced with kind permission of the Governing Body of Lady Margaret Hall, Oxford)*
13) The River Cherwell above Marston Ferry in 1885 *(By courtesy of Oxfordshire County Council Photographic Archive)*
14) Marston looking North along Oxford Road c1885 *(By courtesy of Oxfordshire County Council Photographic Archive)*
15) A College Group in 1886 *(Reproduced with kind permission of the Governing Body of Lady Margaret Hall, Oxford)*
16) A College Group in 1887 *(Reproduced with kind permission of the Governing Body of Lady Margaret Hall, Oxford)*
17) A College Group in 1888 *(Reproduced with kind permission of the Governing Body of Lady Margaret Hall, Oxford)*
18) Drama Group 1887 *(Reproduced with kind permission of the Governing Body of Lady Margaret Hall, Oxford)*
19) Miss Elizabeth Wordsworth in 1909 *(Reproduced with kind permission of the Governing Body of Lady Margaret Hall, Oxford)*
22) Cousins in 1895 *(By courtesy of Miss Dormer Gutch)*
23) Dalmeny Avenue, Islington c1905. *(Courtesy of the London Borough of Islington - Libraries)*
24) James and Ada Murray and family *(Courtesy of Oxford University Press)*
25) James Murray in the Scriptorium *(Courtesy of Oxford University Press)*
26) Joseph Wright *(Courtesy of the National Portrait Gallery, London)*
28) Dr Furnivall *(Courtesy of Oxford University Press)*
29) Leamington Library PH350/1269 *(Source: Warwickshire County Record Office)*
31) Ellen Dykes *(From the collection of Kathleen Hanks)*
32/33) The Leet Book page and exterior *(By permission of Coventry City Council)*

Illustrations not listed are from the collection of the author.

1. BACKGROUND AND EARLY LIFE

Mary Dormer Harris had a background that was so thoroughly steeped in Warwickshire history that it was small wonder that she chose to spend most of her life writing about Warwickshire's past. On both sides her family were gentleman farmers, mostly tenants of farms owned by Lord Leigh. Great-grandfathers, grandfathers, uncles and various cousins, had paid their rent each Michaelmas and Lady Day for centuries and made enough money to pay the farmworkers and have enough left for a reasonably good standard of living for themselves. It was very much a privileged middle-class background, and in each household there would have been at least one domestic servant, who might also have helped with the lighter farm duties.

The two farms which were connected with the family more than any others were the Dale House, Stoneleigh, and the Dial House, Ashow, near the bridge over the Avon at Chesford. Dial House Farm still exists much as it did in the past, as does Dale House, close to the Finham Brook, off Dalehouse Lane to the north west of Kenilworth. At one time MDH's family also used to be the tenants of Kingswood Farm, on the other side of Dale House Lane.

MDH was born into a rural world, which preserved much of the framework of mediaeval times, in which tenant farmers farmed the same land that their forebears had tilled for many generations. So perhaps it was small wonder that she developed into one of the most able mediaeval scholars Warwickshire has ever had.

BIRTHPLACE - DALE HOUSE FARM, STONELEIGH

"And never, though I have envied the ability and achievement of others, 'desiring that man's art and that man's scope' never have I for one moment envied any man his birthplace; my own was so fair."

So said MDH in an article on the village of Stoneleigh, published a few years before her death.

Her maternal grandmother had gone to Dale House as a bride in the 1820s and her mother been born in the house. Both grandfathers had farmed there at various times and her father had moved to Dale House when a young man of twenty-six. Before she was ever properly conscious of her surroundings, she must have absorbed the extraordinary stability of that home situation.

In the same article, written late in life, MDH recalled the magic of the house.

"To some folk it might appear just an old red house, overgrown with ivy and creepers; to me it has the air of Paradise. Within are all manner of quirks and corners, passages and hidey-holes where children can play. In the middle of the hall

DALE HOUSE FARM, NEAR KENILWORTH, WHERE MARY DORMER HARRIS WAS BORN IN 1867.

is a tall wooden pillar like an ancient roof-tree. In a dark garret - some windows had been blocked up in the days of the tax - sweet-smelling apples lay half-smothered in the straw. In what we called the mangle-room, with the concrete floor, I think in old time they stored the cheeses. I can just remember the beer brewing in a huge copper in the scullery. Close by it, was the deep oven we heated with wood in the strenuous days of November, when all hands were turned to the making and filling of pork pies. The kitchen, with red-quarried floor, was a long room warmed by two fires, the walls lined with dark-wood drawers and cupboards, and on an old round table of Spanish chestnut I once saw the Kenilworth tailor sitting cross-legged, as men of his calling do in fairy tales."

BIRTH IN 1867

MDH was born on 11th August 1867 at a time when many things were changing. The Second Reform Bill gave the vote to all adult males with an established place of residence and although philosopher John Stuart Mill urged the idea of Women's Suffrage, this had little support. During her life-time MDH was to fight hard for this cause and it would seem that this same struggle was with her from the month of her birth.

During 1867 many exciting developments took place. Joseph Lister adopted new antiseptic surgical methods and Alfred Nobel (whose fortune afterwards funded various international prizes) demonstrated dynamite. In London in 1867 the building of the Royal Albert Hall began and Thomas Barnardo founded the East End Mission for destitute children. Yet in rural areas many ideas from past centuries lingered on and in Warwick drunken men were still being put in movable stocks on wheels, which were positioned in the Market Hall when required.

BAPTISM IN THE SAME CHURCH AS BOTH OF HER PARENTS

MDH was baptised in St Mary's Church, Stoneleigh, on September 8th 1867. Having been born at nearby Fletchamstead, her father Thomas, son of Thomas and Elizabeth Harris, had been baptised in the same church on May 3rd 1832.

MDH's mother had also been baptised at Stoneleigh. The daughter of Joseph and Elizabeth Dormer of Dale House Farm, she was baptised on May 29th 1834. As if to emphasize the lifelong family friendship between the Harrises and the Dormers, in the register of Stoneleigh Church, after the baptisms of MDH's parents, came James Harris, the younger brother of her father, on May 7th 1835, and James Alfred Dormer, the younger brother of her mother, on October 18th 1838. However the Harris and Dormer families were not that unusual because family involvement in the same area was very much a characteristic of rural communities in the mid-nineteenth century.

It would appear that her father's parents had both died several years before MDH was born. One Thomas Harris died in 1865 aged 65 and his wife had died at the same age in 1861. However in families where father and son and mother and

JAMES ALFRED DORMER (1838 - 1917) WAS AN UNCLE OF MARY DORMER HARRIS. He lived at Dial House Farm, Ashow for much of his life and married again after his first wife died young, leaving him with one son.

daughter often shared the same name, it is easy to make mistakes when consulting contemporary records.

Preliminary studies of the Harris and Dormer families in mid-Warwickshire seem to suggest that MDH's parents were cousins and indeed such unions were quite common in the nineteenth century. However, for anyone with time to spare, the family tree of the Dormers, Harrises, Garners and Garrards would provide occupation for a long time, as there had been much inter-marrying and there were numerous family members with identical or similar names. It should be stressed that the Dormer family to which MDH's mother belonged had no direct connection with the family of Lord Dormer of Grove Park. However there probably was a link to the family of George Eliot (born Mary Ann Evans, near Nuneaton, in 1819) for the famous novelist had an aunt on her mother's side named Mrs Garner.

In taking her mother's maiden name of Mary Dormer, coupled with her father's surname of Harris, the subject of this book was given a name, common enough in her own extended family, but to the world at large, a fine-sounding and distinguished one. In her early life she was often known as plain Mary or Molly Harris, exactly like her mother, but from her twenties onwards the usual form was Miss Dormer Harris.

THOMAS GARNER HARRIS

Around fifteen months after MDH's birth, she had a baby brother, who was, like her, born at Dale House Farm and named after parents and grandparents. Thomas Garner Harris was baptised on 8th November 1868, taking his maternal grandmother's maiden name as his second name. Great must have been the rejoicing in the family for with a beautiful home and two children, a girl and a boy, the Harris family must have seemed secure and happy.

There is no doubt from what she wrote afterwards that MDH loved having a younger brother, *"my little playmate"* as she called him tenderly.

As MDH grew up with her younger brother as company she had some very happy times. Many of these were described in a essay "The Old Farm House".

Her first childhood memory was of when she was three years old being ill in the best room that fronted the rosy eastern sun at Dale House.

"Brown holland hangings, trimmed with red braid, hid the flowery curtains, and on the mantlepiece stood the white artificialities that had crowned my mother's wedding cake and the glass with strips of coloured sand from Alum Chine. One day when I was better and Dr Clark stood smiling by the bed, dear and most comfortable hands wrapped me in a blanket and bore me to the window, so that I might see the drum and fife band below on the garden path, playing their Christmas tunes as the custom was."

Often MDH and her little brother would play together outside the house. The wagon shed, containing brightly painted carts *"with iron-shod wheels,"* could be used to play house.

"Two or three playmates can thus furnish their habitations, people them with families, and pay calls on one another the livelong day."

The singed carcase of the household pig that used to hang from a hook in the ceiling of the dairy caused an observant comment: MDH said she did not mind passing by the body of the animal, but her little brother objected very much. *"He would travel from front room to kitchen by devious ways, through passages, up one flight of stairs and down another, for fear the open dairy door, as he passed, should reveal the horror within."*

Perhaps to children unused to keeping domestic animals, this seems rather a pointless exercise but few today have to eat animals which were previously petted and stroked when they were fed daily, often by the children of the family. In Victorian England however, there was no place for sentiment over the domestic fowls or family pig. When the time came, a few weeks before Christmas, the pig would be led up the garden path and slaughtered on the spot by the visiting pig-killer. Perhaps young Thomas Harris had heard the squeals of the poor pig before it was humanely despatched; this might account for his horror of passing the body.

Once Thomas fell into some weedy water at the bottom of a slope. MDH wrote,

"Ah! I can see him now, as kind and comforting hands lead him up the lawn; bitterly he weeps, and his pinafore is charged with small creatures of the slime."

Sadly having a wonderful house in which to grow up does not guarantee happiness and what memories there were became tinged with sadness for in the summer of 1873, when MDH was just a few weeks short of her sixth birthday, tragedy struck the happy family in the Dale House.

A FUNERAL ON JULY 25TH 1873

The sad happenings of that hot July in 1873 can best be described by MDH herself. A tender paragraph conveyed happenings almost too terrible to remember.

Speaking of the farmhouse, MDH wrote,

"When you reach the upper floor the passage will lead you to the great cool chamber over the dairy looking north where I faintly remember an orange-curtained bed. In one corner a tall, curtained shower bath stood. It never seemed to me to be a homely place. Into the coolness they brought my playmate, whom the gods loved, during the heat of a sultry July. There was coming and going for a day or two, then he lay quite still. Careful women came and laid pennies on his eyelids to close his eyes. I do not think I felt; I only remember. That is all."

A family mourning card tells us that Thomas Garner Harris died on July 23rd 1873 and the burial records of Stoneleigh Church tell that he was buried two days later on July 25th. The little boy was a few months short of his fifth birthday.

Years later, it was said by a family friend that he died from having a fish-bone, or some other obstruction, lodged in his throat, but how true this is I do not know. Whatever ailed him, his death was rather sudden for in the same essay,

MDH referred to him as crossing the hall of the farm house, clad in his sailor suit, on the last market Saturday *"...when the shadows had begun to close around him."*

A LONELY TIME

From that time on, MDH had rather a lonely life at Dale House Farm. She continued to play outside but her games were ones which a solitary child with a vivid imagination could play. She watched the farm labourers as they cut mangolds or threshed the corn and the barn *"where mote-peopled sunbeams fell on golden straw"* was a source of delight. The shrubbery gate was good to swing on and the shutters of the house were a marvellous fascination.

In many ways the garden sounded quite idyllic.

"The deodars in the garden will make lovely sounds for you with the breeze in their branches, and the willows by the water's edge will turn silver white in shimmering changeful beauty as the wind passes by. It is well to come in flowering-time to see the garden, which I tell you is enchanted ground."

Away from the garden the rural setting was magnificent with stepping stones, purple orchids and an oak tree whose *"hospitable forked branches furnish little climbers with a pleasant seat upon a summer's day."*

It is quite clear that from an early age MDH was aware of the natural beauty of the earth and I like to imagine her, aged ten maybe, sitting in the branches of her favourite oak, with a good book or perhaps just watching the sky and listening to the birds singing. Like many Victorian children she loved tales of fairies and when she

THE BACK OF DALE HOUSE. As a rather solitary child, Mary Dormer Harris often played alone in the large garden. (Photograph taken in 1979 on a visit by the Memorial Bursary Trustees.)

described the pit-hole, west of Dale House, she told how the fairies had *"inherited this cup like hollow, with the little pit at the bottom, a little red clayey path at its side, and banks, 'where oxlips and nodding violet grows.'"*

A vivid picture of life on a mid Warwickshire farm emerges from her essay as MDH observed,

"...if it is Friday, the farmer may be sitting by the long white table with a little soiled money-bag before him and piles of silver coin. The ruddy-faced spare men come in one by one; they shuffle out into the twilight, "passing rich" or poor on a thirteen shillings weekly wage. Meanwhile tea is spread in the dining room, with pork pie baked in hot wood embers, and well stuffed chine. And when the meal is over, a child can listen in the lamplight to stories, endless stories, - stories of thieves and witches, of birds and beasts..."

FAMILY STORIES. MURDER AND GUNPOWDER.

As she grew up in Stoneleigh, apart from the time when she was attending a private school, MDH was largely in the company of her mother and other adults. Family visits were frequent and at family gatherings, tales of past misdemeanours and troubles were related again.

One of the most horrific of these family stories was of how her great-grandmother had been murdered in 1819 in the nearby village of Ashow. In her article entitled "Ashow," MDH recounted the horrific story.

"It was because permission to go to the Wake was refused her that Ann Heytrey, a servant girl, murdered her mistress, Mrs Sarah Dormer, on August 29th 1819 at the Dial House, Ashow. The account of the trial in the Warwick Advertiser of April 15th 1820 makes painful reading. According to the indictment, the girl "being moved and seduced by the instigation of the Devil," had traitorously murdered her mistress with a certain knife to the value of 6d... Among the witnesses were three girls, my grand mother and her sisters, daughters of the dead woman. The accused persisted that she had no motive for the act, that her mistress had never given her an angry word; it is charitable to suppose that, unbalanced in mind and worn out with work, she was seized with an access of mania. She wrote a letter, still possessed by the family, imploring forgiveness. Of course she was publicly hanged. An old woman at Ashow, long dead, used to relate her disappointment because, being unwell, her mother would not let her accompany her brothers to witness the sight, for parents then sent youngsters to watch public executions - as a warning to them to avoid the commission of crimes!"

In her book "Warwickshire Murders" Betty Smith gives a longer account. Indeed over the years this murder has become particularly well-known in Warwickshire, perhaps because the details were very gory indeed.

Another true family story concerned her maternal grandmother who had come to Dale House when a bride in the 1820s. Again a newspaper cutting, this time from the "Courier" of December 27th 1828.

"CAUTION. On Thursday se'enight a melancholy accident happened to Mrs Dormer, of the Dale house, near Stonley. Mr D. had been out shooting rabbits, and on his return left his gun loaded in the kitchen, when it was accidentally knocked down, and unfortunately the whole charge lodged in the foot of Mrs Dormer, who was sitting by the fire, and, it is feared, will be obliged to submit to amputation."

Happily her grandmother escaped this fate which would have been carried out without anaesthetic or antiseptics and, although she was *"at death's door"* for a time, she eventually recovered and discarded her crutches.

The same grandparents had had trouble two months previously when Mr Dormer had placed a quantity of gunpowder in the oven to dry and the whole thing had exploded while he was away at church. Although he had remembered what he had done and rushed out of the service, before he had arrived home the explosion had occurred.

However life with Grandfather Dormer had many lighter moments and once a policeman, who had come to court the housemaid, was doused with a pail of dirty water because it was thought he was an intruder.

GRANDMOTHER

The grandmother who had endured much in her early life had another trauma to suffer in her old age for she went blind. In an essay "Grandmother" MDH gave a vivid description of the rather stern old lady who filled her grandchildren with awe.

"....The brown eyes turned towards you were dull and sightless, and the once so tireless hands, now brown and incredibly wrinkled, with the wedding ring embedded in the third finger, lay perforce idle on her silk apron... There comes to my mind a picture of her seated figure in the back room of a little town house where the light seemed hardly to penetrate from the window which gave on a little dark-pavemented garden. But all surroundings are alike to those who cannot behold the sun."

One of the few pleasures which her grandmother had in her later years was being read to and MDH would often read the poems of Milton to her. She enjoyed "Paradise Lost" because Milton too had been blind.

The death of the old lady at Dale House Farm was quiet and sad.

"Her end came quietly in extreme old age as she lay in the little green parlour of the house to which she had come more than sixty years before as a bride, murmuring with dying lips the ancient words millions have spoken "O Thou, who hearest prayer, to thee all flesh shall come."

A CLEVER WOMAN

In many ways her maternal grandmother is important in the life of MDH for she had been an extremely clever young woman. In her youth she had attended the school in Nuneaton which for many years was kept by Mrs Wallington and years later, George Eliot had attended this same school. MDH observed *"Mrs Wallington's daughter Mrs Buchanan is famed as the tragic heroine of 'Janet's*

Repentance'". When at the Nuneaton school her grandmother often saw Mr and Mrs Everard, George Eliot's uncle and aunt.

MDH gave a vivid picture of her grandmother in her younger days,

"As a housewife grandmother fell short of success, but attractive-looking she certainly was...Undoubtedly she was the clever woman of the family, and she remained at school longer than her sisters."

It would appear that this cleverness and dislike of housework showed itself again in Elizabeth Dormer's granddaughter Mary.

MOTHER

MDH's mother, Mary Dormer, was born at Dale House Farm in 1834 and she became a hardworking and practical person, unlike her mother and daughter who were more intellectual and bookish. Like others in the Dormer family, she had a beautiful singing voice and she appears to have been an accomplished pianist.

Just as her mother had been, Mary Dormer was well-educated and at the age of fourteen *"she was sent to "finish" at Miss Blair's school, now Abbey House on the Abbey Hill , a school of good repute."*

A fascinating picture of the Kenilworth in which her mother grew up is given by MDH in an essay "Kenilworth in the Forties." Imagining the scene she writes,

"The tilbury is at the door. We are to drive to Mrs Pope's of Castle End, to take tea. Maybe we shall encounter on the road kind old Dr Obadiah Ayton, astride his chestnut cob, Mr Pickwick to the life, but hiding his bald pate under a tawny wig, made adhesive above the ears by visible patches of cobbler's wax. We may also pass Ned Grizzle, the rag-and-bone man from Albion Row, in his little cart, a sinister figure with a club foot and club hand. Ugh! How he belabours his donkey with the whip held in the hand he can use freely, while the reins are wrapped round his twisted wrist."

Going on to describe the congregation in St Nicholas Church, Kenilworth, with Sir John and Lady Browne-Cave and their daughters Rosalie, Louisa and Hyacinth, Mr Draper the tanner, Mrs Mayer with her bevy of daughters, a builder named Robbins and the De La Bere Barkers, old bachelors who lived in the house with the long portico on Abbey Hill, MDH makes the history seem alive and personal. We can easily visualize Luke Starley the parish-clerk in the lowest seat of the three-decker, with his wig and open prayer-book, ready to deliver a forcible Amen! at the proper place.

Perhaps the most vivid character of the Kenilworth of a hundred and fifty years ago is that of Mrs Turner, a cobbler's wife who lived in Mile End. Not only did Mrs Turner char for Mrs Dormer at the Dale House, but every Friday, for 10 pence a day, she walked to Coventry and back to sell the Dale House butter and eggs in the Women's Market. Mrs Turner, in her well-worn shawl and coal-scuttle bonnet, often battling against wind and rain, seemed to personify the hard life experienced by many of the lowly-paid in Victorian times.

FATHER

Thomas Harris had been born in Fletchamstead in 1832 and he had lived much of his early life there. MDH gave a good summary of his life in her newspaper article on Stoneleigh.

"My father, who must have started farming at the Dale House about 1858, lived a care-free life of country sports and jollity; rather in the spirit of the young people of Shakespeare's comedies until a cloud of anxiety overcast his sky."

Like many farmers, her father appeared to be especially keen on shooting, often attended by Flash, *"the brown and white curly-eared spaniel."* On 1st March 1861, Thomas Harris had won a silver cup, presented by Lord Leigh, for clay-pigeon shooting.

Unfortunately in the 1870s farming in England suffered many problems as cheap American corn flooded in. The price of wheat and other crops fell through the floor. MDH explained,

"The American prairies were sown with corn; ships of unprecedented size bore bumper harvests across the sea, and wheat which had touched record prices during the Crimean War, fell in the 'seventies almost to nothing. My father tried many things to retrieve the old prosperity. He hoped much from some land-working invention of his displayed at the Coventry Agricultural Show. He planted fruit trees; he essayed market gardening, but though he could help others to fortune he could not make his own. A man of great gifts, "a fellow of infinite jest" whose conversation was everywhere welcome, he just lacked the more everyday qualities which make for success."

In many ways it would seem that MDH herself took after her father and it was obviously from him that she inherited her great sense of humour. However the description of her father ends with the sad sentence,

"He laid down the burden of life when I was little more than a child."

Actually MDH was fourteen when her father died on 7th February 1882. Presumably he had been ill for his will was made just a couple of weeks beforehand. It was a simple will, executed at home, naming his wife as sole beneficiary.

The Warwick Advertiser for 11th February 1882 had a tiny obituary notice which read,

"On 7th Instant, at Dale House, Kenilworth, Thomas Harris, aged 49 years. Will friends kindly accept this notice."

Like his young son of the same name, Thomas Harris was buried at Stoneleigh and young Mary and her mother, aged forty eight, were left to pick up the pieces of their lives.

MRS HARRIS RUNS THE FARM

The death of Thomas Harris was not recorded officially in the rental accounts of the Leigh Estate. In the Accounts Book for Lady Day 1882, the entry merely read,

"Received from the Executors of Thomas Harris £331 5sh" being the half

yearly rent for Dale House and Kingswood farms.

In the arrears column it was written that he had died owing arrears of rent of £115 17 3d but that this was *"Excused under Lord Leigh's instructions"*.

Obviously this was a kindly gesture from Lord Leigh for the family of a long-established tenant. It probably meant that Mrs Harris did not need to sell any of the family possessions in order to pay the debt. Officially Thomas Harris's personal estate was worth £2,672 but it seems likely that most, if not all, of this amount was in the form of household items, farm-stock and equipment.

Given this chance to start afresh, Mrs Harris then took over the farm herself and for the next eight years she is listed as being the tenant. Although she had been born on the farm and knew it well, the actual running of the business must have been difficult for in 1883 an entry in the Account Books recorded that she paid a reduced rent as *"Kingswood had been given up."*

Mrs Harris continued as the tenant until around 1890 when MDH said that her folks left Dale House.

2. EDUCATION

A PRIVATE SCHOOL FOR GIRLS

At what age I do not know, perhaps from the age of five or six, Mary Dormer Harris was sent to a small school run by Mrs McEwan in Kenilworth. White & Co's 1874 Directory for Warwickshire informs us that Mrs M. E. McEwan lived in "Ivy Bank" Ladies Hills, which was close to the Kenilworth end of Dale House Lane. So MDH would not have had far to travel to school.

In those times there were many small private schools, held in private houses, and it is more than likely that Mrs McEwan's school was of this variety and that it had only a handful of pupils. It would have been unthinkable in those class-conscious Victorian times for the daughter of a gentleman-farmer to be educated alongside the children of farm labourers, so there would have been no question of her attending the village school at Stoneleigh. Some girls were educated at home, but this would have meant that she had little daily contact with other children and, in any case, Mrs McEwan was apparently well-respected in scholastic circles.

In an essay on "George Eliot" written many years later, MDH mentions a Mrs

MY DEAREST
MOTHER
I HOPE YOU
ARE QUITE WELL
AND PAPA TOO.
MY LOVE TO ALL
YOUR LOVING
DAUGHTER
MARY

AN EARLY PIECE OF WRITING BY YOUNG MDH, POSSIBLY COMPLETED IN HER FIRST SCHOOL IN KENILWORTH WHEN SHE WAS AGED FIVE OR SIX.

McEwan, who was presumably the teacher of her young days. It was said that her husband had taught music to George Eliot at some time, and certainly Mrs McEwan herself had knowledge of various people from Nuneaton whom the novelist described in her books. It is pure quess-work on my part but in her younger days, Mrs McEwan may well have attended Mrs Wallington's School in Nuneaton as did both MDH's grandmother and George Eliot.

BOARDING-SCHOOL LIFE

Some time later, perhaps after the death of her father in 1882, when her mother was running the farm, MDH left Warwickshire and went to the Richmond and Twickenham High School, a private boarding school for young ladies near London. Archive material concerning her schooldays is very scanty, but late in life MDH did write an essay "Felbrigg Villa" which appeared to describe the Richmond School with the names of the teachers and the name of the house changed. From the essay we learn that MDH's cousin Maria was also a pupil. However although Maria stayed at school at weekends, MDH was only a weekly boarder and it may have been that she stayed with relations in London at weekends.

STAYING WITH THE SAVAGE FAMILY IN ISLINGTON

On July 11th 1874 Louisa Garner of Wasperton Hill, aged 31, married Thomas Savage, aged 38, then living at an address in Gloucester Road, Regent's Park, London. It seems likely that Louisa was a cousin of MDH's mother. By 1881 Thomas Savage was a Professor of Mathematics and he and his wife and young children were living at 2 St Bartholomew Road, Islington (after 1894 renamed Dalmeny Avenue).

In 1894 MDH gave her official address as 2 Dalmeny Avenue, but taking into account all the circumstances, it would seem highly likely that her close association with her London relations began far earlier, in fact when she first attended the girls' boarding school in Twickenham. Furthermore, since he obviously had considerable knowledge of higher education, Professor Thomas Savage may well have given valuable advice to MDH and her mother.

RICHMOND AND TWICKENHAM HIGH SCHOOL

The Kelly's Directory of 1887/88 records the Richmond and Twickenham High School as being held in a house called Bathurst Lodge in Park Road, St Margaret's, Twickenham, the road later being renamed St George's Road. The Misses Cookson were listed as the occupants. A peep at the exterior of Bathurst Lodge today, almost hidden behind tall trees, gives you a glimpse of an elegant house, which would fit the *"square, sedate, stucco building"* described in "Felbrigg Villa" very well. Many of the houses in the near vicinity had an air of faded Victorian grandeur and it was easy to imagine MDH and other middle-class young ladies being educated in such an environment.

FELBRIGG VILLA

The school as described by MDH in retrospect, sounded exactly like so many others of the time.

"Compared with modern standards the education imparted at Felbrigg Villa, a school kept by three ageing sisters - even then deemed old fashioned - was quite deplorable, but who then, save a few despised pioneers, gave a thought to girls' intellectual development?"

The environment seems to have been very spartan. *"Bedclothes, as one crept shiveringly between them in the darkness of the top-bedroom at Felbrigg Villa were glacial to a degree beyond all present experience....water commonly froze in one's jug and basin..."* The food at the school was similarly basic and consisted mainly of bread and butter, except for dinner which was slightly more generous.

For exercise the girls were taken on a mid-day "crocodile" walk and occasionally in summer they were allowed to take a hoop or ball into the neighbouring avenues for a run after breakfast. Only the ball had to be thrown up and caught, not bounced, in case by bending the girls developed a tendency to stoop which was *"a consummation to be avoided at all costs."* It seems the pupils had to spend some time laying down on a backboard and part of the exercise routine was for two lines of girls to practise bowing to each other; this being an activity they would need to conduct perfectly in later life.

The quality of the education did not sound to be very great and MDH said *"We learnt French from a pleasant little stout, lorgon-wearing Mademoiselle through the medium of perfectly hopeless books."* Although the girls were taught a little arithmetic, this was not readily understood from the inadequate instruction and MDH confessed that she never did master compound division.

In the last paragraph of the essay MDH states one of the eternal truths concerning school and it rather suggests that much of what she learned in life was self-taught later on.

"...Compared with life all teachers seem of a futility - and by the side of the discovery of our own natures no lesson seems of the slightest import."

"CHRISTIE'S OLD ORGAN"

The school in Twickenham did have its lighter moments and like many Victorian children MDH was brought up on the moral stories as described in the numerous cheap religious tracts published in the 1880s. She wrote,

"I can also recall pleasant evenings when the upper schoolroom was warmed by light and fire, and Miss Janet read aloud some moving story of child-life in the East End of London, "Froggie's Little Brother" or "Christies Old Organ." Dear Miss Janet! I can see her now in her round white cap with cap strings of purple ribbon, her mild brown eyes obscured by tinted glasses, laughing gently behind an upraised hand at some of Christie's or Froggie's sallies of wit."

When I first read MDH's memories of "Christies Old Organ" I was delighted

WHEN AT A BOARDING-SCHOOL IN TWICKENHAM IN THE 1880s, MARY DORMER HARRIS RECALLED THE RELIGIOUS TRACT "CHRISTIES OLD ORGAN" BEING READ TO THE OLDER PUPILS. This engraving forms the frontispiece to that book and clearly illustrates the organ referred to in the tear-jerking story.

for our family has a well-worn copy of this same book. It was, I believe, given to my great-grandfather in the days of his youth and my late mother recalled reading passages of the book aloud to her aged great-aunt in the 1920s. I treasure our copy still and can readily understand the strict moral code of MDH's schooldays when I inspect its simple engravings.

VISIT TO FRANCE AND GERMANY IN 1884

Two very interesting communications still exist which MDH wrote to her widowed mother in 1884. MDH visited France and Germany and a post-card, clearly dated July 1884, and a letter, almost certainly written the following day, throw much light on the teenage girl who was learning to make witty and pertinent comments about her surroundings.

The post-card was sent from Rosstrappe, and the letter from Gernrode, both places in the Harz mountains of Northern Germany.

Since my knowledge of the area was almost nil, I was extremely grateful for information imparted by Mrs Hildegard Hughes, a friend who lived in the same area

THE LEGEND OF ROSSTRAPPE AS ILLUSTRATED ON A POST-CARD MARY DORMER HARRIS SENT HER MOTHER FROM GERMANY IN 1884. In the legend the beautiful Brunhilde, on her faithful horse, was able to cross the steep ravine, but her pursuer, a giant named Bodo, fell. Postcards with similar illustrations are still sold today.

of Germany when young. She has now lived in Leamington for many years, but as I described the letter and card in which MDH wrote of the Harz Mountains area in glowing terms, Mrs Hughes looked wistful and said, yes, they were truly beautiful.

The post card sent in 1884 had an engraving in the corner of the card depicting the interesting legend attached to the steep-sided valley, near Rosstrappe and Mrs Hughes assured me that similar cards were still being sold today. A beautiful maiden, Brunhilde, was being pursued by a giant she disliked intensely, but who was supposed to marry her. She ran away on the eve of their wedding and her horse successfully jumped across a ravine to safety, but the horse of Bodo the giant fell, pitching him into the ravine. From that time onwards the river has been known as the Boder.

The letter is undated, but was obviously written just after the post-card. The address given is the Haus Hagenthal, near Gernrode, in the Harz, and it would appear from the content that MDH had travelled with a Mrs Wheeler and her daughter Kathleen. Typical of a teenage girl, MDH uses the quirky "2" throughout, instead of the words "two" or "to."

"My dear mother,

I have such a lot to tell you about the Harz. They are so lovely. I never would have believed there could be anything so lovely under the sun as the Bodethal...

QUEDLINBURG, IN THE HARZ MOUNTAINS OF GERMANY, WHICH MDH VISITED IN 1884. It was in the picturesque towns of northern Germany, in particular Hildesheim, that she first began to appreciate old buildings.

On Thursday morning we started at 7 rather early mother even for you, considering we have a 20 minute walk 2 the station. We were a pretty large party (?) all English consisting of 4 Miss Lords, the Wheelers and myself."

After the Miss Lords had gone to a hotel nearby, MDH gives a hilarious description of the jolting experienced on an omnibus drive from Quedlinburg Station to the hotel in Hagenthal where she and Wheelers were to stay.

"Oh the jolting of that omnibus drive - it was indescribable. The Germans always pave their roads with petrified potatoes and the jolting thereof may you never experience it my mother. There were a good many people in the omnibus and it was a trifle stuffy. We were boiling when a woman asked us to shut one window , but she was not content until we had shut the other so destroying our last hope of a refreshing breeze. I am a thorough Harris not a Dormer as you know and cannot bear stuffy rooms, like some of my near relations (maternal). When we got to Hagenthal there were nearly all the guests assembled not to welcome but to stare at us... Our rooms are very nice and we have a lovely view from our window of woods and hills. At supper we summoned up courage 2 go and eat at the Table D'hote, (70 people) but found not a soul to speak to for the people knowing that we were English and not knowing that at least Kathleen and I could speak a little German fled from us as if we had the plague. That astonished me as I found Germans are so sociable..."

Of the little town of Gernrode MDH wrote,

"It is such an old little town and nearly all the bigger houses are painted light green and salmon colour....At dinner I summoned up courage to address my neighbour in German and we soon got up a conversation about the weather. In the evening we paid the Miss Lords a visit in their hotel, congratulating ourselves that we were not staying there because our view is so much prettier. I have never enjoyed myself so much for years as I did yesterday. I will tell you about it."

Sadly the next page of the letter is missing and we are left to conjecture what the experience might have been.

To my shame I queried the remark about the *"petrified potatoes"* but Mrs Hughes assured me that years ago brown cobbles were used to pave the streets of the Gernrode area. So MDH was making a very fair comparison.

HILDESHEIM

In an interview with a newspaper in 1911 MDH confessed that her interest in old buildings dated back to her visit to the old German town of Hildesheim. Presumably MDH and her companion visited that town on the same trip in 1884, which also took in places in France. It would seem that the main purpose of the travel was to improve the fluency of their spoken French and German.

I am lucky enough to own a set of Encyclopaedia Britannica of 1882 and from the entry on the town of Hildesheim, near Hanover, it seems small wonder that MDH came to love its old buildings.

The Encyclopaedia said the town had *"an antique and quaint"* appearance and old ramparts had been converted into shady alleys and promenades. The narrow and irregular streets had old houses with over-hanging upper stories and the Roman Catholic Cathedral dated from the middle of the eleventh century. In the ancient Cathedral was a font dating to the thirteenth century and candelabra to the twelfth century, whilst the rose bush on the wall of the crypt was said to be a thousand years old.

Reading through the description in the 1882 Enclopaedia, the similarities between Hildesheim and Coventry became obvious. It would appear that the valuable experience of seeing another historical town in another country gave MDH a clearer idea of the larger historical picture.

LADY MARGARET HALL, OXFORD

When she was eighteen MDH took the Cambridge Higher Local examinations, perhaps under the guidance of Professor Thomas Savage who may have arranged suitable tuition for her. She obtained English Class Two, with Distinction in General Literature, and History Class Two, with Distinction in Political History. On the strength of these results she was accepted at Lady Margaret Hall, Oxford, to study English.

In those early days there were no formal examinations for entry and the teaching of all the students in the female colleges was arranged through the Association of Education for Women.

Lady Margaret Hall, the first of the women's colleges in Oxford, was founded in 1878, opened in 1879 and run along Church of England lines. Elizabeth Wordsworth, the daughter of the Bishop of Lincoln, was the first Principal and in 1886, when MDH entered, there were between 25 and 30 students living in a large house, with some extra buildings, in Norham Gardens, Oxford.

Fortunately the college had a tradition of a group photograph each year and so MDH features on three such groups. In 1886 a rather shy-looking, short-sighted girl, her glasses hanging on a cord at her side, kept her eyes demurely away from the camera. In 1887 and 1888 a more confident-looking, bespectacled young woman appears on the photographs.

LIFE IN OXFORD 1886-1888

In 1884 Lady Margaret Hall had had a new building and a chapel had been added in 1886. Life for the students was far from easy and when they wished to go out, they were encouraged to go *"Two or three together."* If they needed to go out in the evenings, chaperones were necessary, and the Principal and senior staff often had a busy time of it. I do not think it ever happened to MDH for she usually went out accompanied by a friend, but sometimes the female students could be observed walking around Oxford with their maids.

In 1886, only seven years after the opening of Lady Margaret Hall and

THIS 1880s VIEW OF THE APPROACH TO OXFORD FROM THE BANBURY ROAD MUST HAVE BEEN VERY FAMILIAR TO MARY DORMER HARRIS IN HER LATE TEENS AND EARLY TWENTIES.

LADY MARGARET HALL, IN NORHAM GARDENS, OXFORD, MUCH AS IT WAS WHEN MARY DORMER HARRIS FIRST WENT UP TO READ ENGLISH IN 1886. During the three years she spent there, the total number of students at any given time rarely exceeded thirty-five.

MARY DORMER HARRIS, AS SHE APPEARED ON THE GROUP PHOTOGRAPH OF LADY MARGARET HALL, OXFORD IN 1886.

Somerville Colleges, opinion in Oxford and elsewhere was still divided on the advisability of higher education for women. Although there was much encouragement from people such as John Ruskin and Sir William Herschel, other prominent men and women were against higher education and the granting of the vote to women.

After the first term or so MDH became friendly with Florence Hayllar who was to become a life-long friend. Florence Hayllar recalled how she and Molly, as she called her, had spent much of their time.

"My memory of her in those days is largely in country scenes about Oxford, so much of which has now disappeared. The villages, and the fields and wood which could be reached by an afternoon's walk from the Hall were our most familiar ground for those endless talks which are a main joy of youth - and how good a talker Molly always was.

Within doors we read a great deal together, poetry -I believe - for the main part, Molly liked to be read aloud to. She would listen with an absorbed, but active attention which broke out from time to time in characteristic exclamation or comment."

Florence Hayllar also expressed the opinion years later that MDH did not find life easy in her early life. It may well have been that as her confidence increased during her time at Oxford she became more and more determined to use her talents wisely and repay some of her mother's great faith in her.

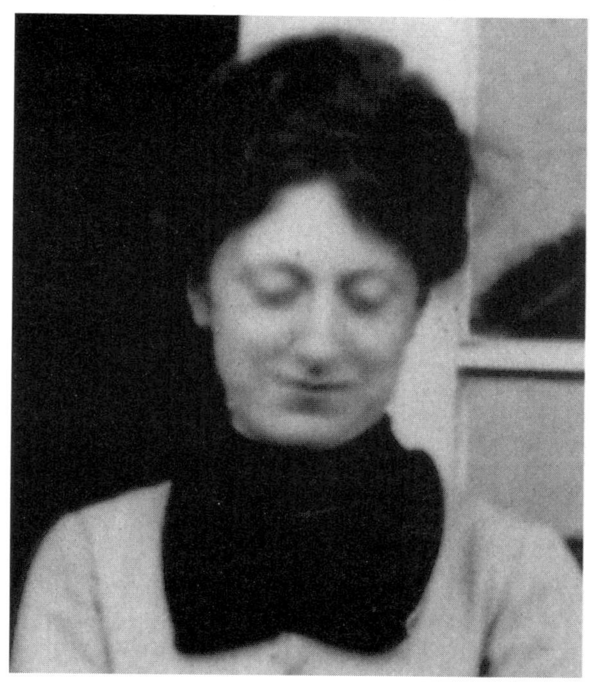

A CLOSE-UP OF FLORENCE HAYLLAR FROM THE HALL GROUP OF 1887

WHEN IN OXFORD, MARY DORMER HARRIS AND FLORENCE HAYLLAR OFTEN TOOK LONG WALKS IN THE AFTERNOONS. They are extremely likely to have visited this spot near the River Cherwell, above Marston Ferry (seen here is a photograph of 1885) for it was not far from their college.

MDH AND FLORENCE HAYLLAR ALSO PROBABLY WALKED THROUGH PICTURESQUE MARSTON VILLAGE. This photograph shows the view looking north along the Oxford Road in 1885.

PLEASE MAY WE HAVE A MIRROR?

The accommodation at Lady Margaret Hall could perhaps best be described as spartan middle-class, which after all was probably what most of the students had been accustomed to in their boarding schools. A delightful petition, which has gone down in the archives of Lady Margaret Hall as the first student protest, took place in 1887. The fact that the students had to ask for such a mirror makes the college sound rather like a nunnery.

The petition read,

"We, the undersigned students of Lady Margaret Hall, find it impossible to keep as tidy as we should wish, without a glass which will reflect more then six square inches at a time. We should therefore be very glad if the Committee would provide a long mirror, to enable us to see ourselves as others see us; and we suggest that it would be an improvement to the drawing room, if placed there between the windows."

The petition was signed by twenty five students, including M. Harris. It is good to relate that the students got their mirror for it came as a gift from Sir William Herschel.

A HALL GROUP IN 1886. TWENTY FIVE STUDENTS ARE PICTURED HERE WITH MARY DORMER HARRIS THE SECOND FROM THE LEFT IN THE FRONT ROW. Miss Wordsworth, the Principal, is in the centre with the white cap, and her assistant E.M. Argles is second from right on the middle row. Gertrude Bell, who afterwards achieved fame as an archaeologist and traveller, is second from right on the front row.

1887 MORE STUDENTS THEN EVER

The college report for the October Term 1887 revealed that there were an increased number of students at Lady Margaret Hall; in fact thirty five in all, the most there had ever been. The accommodation was packed full and a few students, MDH amongst them, were boarded out at St Hugh's, an additional Hall (later to become a separate college) founded in 1886 by Elizabeth Wordsworth, the Principal of Lady Margaret Hall and originally intended to accommodate poorer students.

A RICH AND VARIED LIFE

For many of the students at Lady Margaret Hall and Somerville in the 1880s, life was more interesting and varied than anything they had experienced in their home towns or at school. Not only were they treated as sensible and trustworthy people, they had the opportunity of joining varied activities with the other female students.

Lady Margaret Hall shared a Debating Society with Somerville and it is tempting to imagine outspoken MDH honing her verbal skills in this group. In after life she was acknowledged to be an exceptionally-gifted lecturer, especially on large and important occasions, and although Florence Hayllar said that she had a slight stammer (like her beloved Charles Lamb) she had a wonderful melodious voice.

A HALL GROUP IN 1887 SHOWS A BESPECTACLED MARY DORMER HARRIS ON THE BACK ROW, EXTREME LEFT. Her great friend Florence Hayllar is in the centre of the back row and Miss Argles is in black in the centre of the group.

THE HALL GROUP IN 1888 HAS A SEVERE-LOOKING MARY DORMER HARRIS, DRESSED IN BLACK, ON THE FRONT ROW, SECOND FROM LEFT. Florence Hayllar is on the right of the front row.

The River Cherwell runs close by the college and from 1885 the college owned a boat for the use of students. The boat was nick-named "The Lady Maggie" and although she never mentioned it, it is more than likely that MDH took advantage of this facility at some time.

STUDENT PLAYS

One of the students at Lady Margaret Hall, Molly du Boulay, wrote a play for performance in 1887 and from the letters of Gertrude Bell (afterwards famous as a traveller, archaeologist, diplomat and writer) we learn that it was a play *"with no men in it, which is a great advantage from the point of view of the Stage Manager."* I am not sure what part MDH was playing but from the surviving photograph she appeared to be enjoying it.

In fact we do know that MDH and many of the other girls enjoyed acting very much and the Principal, Miss Wordsworth, encouraged them in this. Sometimes she wrote end of term plays herself and encouraged her students to join her in impromptu readings and charades. This enjoyment of acting was to remain with

MDH for the rest of her life, and in later life she wrote a number of short plays and was a founder member of a local dramatic study club.

THE INSPIRATION OF MISS WORDSWORTH

By all accounts Elizabeth Wordsworth was a remarkable woman and most attribute much of the early success of Lady Margaret Hall to her influence. Not only was she a good organizer, but the students had a great respect for her and often came back to visit her long after they had left.

Miss Wordsworth was very well-educated for a female of her era. Born on June 22nd 1840, she and her family lived in Leamington for a short period around 1845; her father being then under the care of Dr Jephson. Her sister Mary (later Trebeck) was born in Leamington in March 1845 and these early recollections would have given Elizabeth Wordsworth a link with MDH when she first enrolled as a student.

As a great-niece of William Wordsworth, Elizabeth Wordsworth had vivid

ALWAYS A KEEN ACTRESS, MARY DORMER HARRIS IS ON THE EXTREME LEFT OF THIS DRAMA GROUP AT LADY MARGARET HALL IN 1887.

MISS ELIZABETH WORDSWORTH, GREAT-NIECE OF THE FAMOUS POET, WAS APPOINTED AS THE FIRST PRINCIPAL OF LADY MARGARET HALL, OXFORD IN NOVEMBER 1878. For thirty years, from the opening of the college in 1879 to her retirement in 1909, she inspired students by the force of her exceptional personality.

memories of travelling to Rydal with the family in 1850 for her father was the poet's literary executor. The widowed Mrs Wordsworth, Dorothy Wordsworth, Mr Quillinan and the Arnolds all figured largely in her memories, which doubtless served to inspire students of English Literature such as MDH.

THE JUBILEE OF QUEEN VICTORIA IN 1887

MDH was a student in 1887 when Elizabeth Wordsworth and other College Heads were invited to Buckingham Palace as part of the celebrations to mark the Jubilee of Queen Victoria. Miss Wordsworth wrote to her sister on June 23rd 1887,

"I think you may like to hear of my adventures of yesterday...I had a ticket for Buckingham Palace..to help present the Women's Jubilee gift to the Queen and travelled up with Miss Shaw Lefevre (Head of Somerville) *to their nice house in Seymour Street.*

There we found Miss Clough, and Miss Welsh, of Girton and we all started together after lunch, Miss Clough and I in the Shaw Lefevres' carriage - was it not kind?- and the other two in a hansom. We got to Buckingham Palace by the entrée door; went through long passages, which, though handsome, struck me as not so grand as Versailles, but much more comfortable....We must have stood about for a good hour, or sat on the yellow damask chairs - we should not have minded some tea!

...At last the Queen sailed in, in her black silk dress and lace cap, with black transparent lace over her arms, which gave her the effect of being in evening dress. She walked down the line, shaking hands here and there...I never saw her look so nice; her smile is charming..."

After the ceremony, the return journey to (Paddington?) Station took several hours because of a huge traffic jam near Hyde Park Corner. Miss Wordsworth concluded, *Poor Miss Clough will, I fear, be quite done up. She is a dear old lady 'nearly the same age as the Queen'......I did not get to Oxford till near midnight...*

The following day, or at the earliest opportunity, I feel sure Miss Wordsworth would have regaled the students with a full account of her visit. For the rest of her life, MDH would often talk about the long-lived monarch, for whom she had a great respect.

A PICNIC AT BOAR'S HILL

Miss Wordsworth sometimes organized outings for her students and the College Minute Book carried a description of a picnic to Boar's Hill in the summer term of 1888. It appeared that *"several old students joined on one of the few fine days of this rainy summer"*. I do not know how many students took part in the picnic or whether any walked, but with perhaps upwards of forty people travelling by carriage in convoy, it must have been a sight to behold.

QUEEN VICTORIA

A FIRM FOUNDATION FOR LIFE

In later life, MDH spoke of the sacrifice and dedication of her mother and how it was thanks to her that she had been able to achieve so much.

Fees for each term at Lady Margaret Hall were £25 for the Hall Charge and on top of this fees for tuition were paid to the Association for the Education of Women. The amount for this varied between £7 per term to £10 if some private tuition had been obtained. Florence Hayllar and another student shared a scholarship in 1887, but these scholarships were very few and far between and MDH did not have one. Who then paid for her education at Oxford University?

We have no means of knowing, but it may have been that her mother, whilst living frugally herself, made the farm pay well enough to save money for MDH's education. Another possibility is that her maternal grandmother gave up her own home and diverted some of the money thus released towards MDH's education. We know that her blind grandmother returned to live at Dale House several years before her death and it would have been entirely in character for MDH's clever mother and grandmother to have given her the chance of higher education which had been denied to them.

SUMMER TERM 1888. FIRST CLASS IN ENGLISH

Although women were not formally awarded degrees until 1920, they were allowed to sit examinations and in the summer of 1888 three of the students from Lady Margaret Hall obtained Firsts. Janet Hogarth obtained a First in Philosophy, Gertrude Bell a First in Modern History and Mary Dormer Harris a First in English. Thus it would appear that MDH became only the second student from her college to obtain a First Class in English. Before the three in 1888, only three other students had obtained Firsts in any school of study at that college according to Bertha J. Johnson in "The History of Lady Margaret Hall."

However, in the 1880s, the Final Honours School of English was not officially recognised and the examinations were classed as "Women's Exams." At the time MDH must have known this, but her education prior to Oxford may not have fitted her for any other Honours School and in any case, since she wanted to be a writer, she probably felt she needed to study Literature.

In "The Letters of Gertrude Bell," first published in 1927, Janet Hogarth (later Mrs Courtney) was quoted when she gave details of the life of the students in 1888. It seems that for the 'viva voce' part of the final examinations, the parents of the candidates were admitted. If she managed to leave the farm and travel to Oxford to attend MDH's 'viva voce', it must have been one of the proudest moments of Mrs Harris's life.

At Lady Margaret Hall, MDH was an exact contemporary of the slightly-younger, red-haired Gertrude Bell, who came from an extremely wealthy, well-connected family. Being attractive and vivacious, her varied social life included many balls and not approving of female emancipation, she often quoted her industrialist father, as in her often-used phrase to end an argument, *"Well you know, my father says..."* Since MDH was an ardent suffragist and both women were outspoken, I can only suppose there were some lively arguments between the two. With perhaps only a dozen students in each year at that time in the college, Mary Dormer Harris and Gertrude Bell must have known each other well.

Some of the early students spent four or even five years on their studies but MDH spent just under three years. Florence Hayllar had a year out in 1888, so her studies were spread over five years before she took a First in Modern Languages in 1890.

3. DOCUMENTS AND DICTIONARIES 1888-1906

TEACHING IN LONDON AND RESEARCHING IN COVENTRY

On leaving Oxford in the summer of 1888 the movements of Mary Dormer Harris are a little uncertain. She probably spent some time with her mother who was still running Dale House Farm, and her college friend Florence Hayllar certainly visited her in Warwickshire.

In the Autumn of 1888 it seems likely that MDH took up a teaching post in Kensington and she probably lived with her relations in Islington. The Minute Book of Lady Margaret Hall simply said that *"Miss Dormer Harris has also obtained work"* and a report later on said she had found work *"for the present in Kensington."*

It was also at this time that MDH began to research the manuscript records of Coventry. She described this period of her life in a newspaper interview in 1914.

"During my holidays - I was teaching at this time - I used to come down to the city, take lodgings, and read up documents in the Treasury, a room in St Mary's Hall, this being before the muniment room was built. The late Mr Thomas Browett

THE TREASURY IN ST MARY'S HALL WHERE MARY DORMER HARRIS SPENT MANY HOURS READING MEDIAEVAL MANUSCRIPTS IN THE EARLY 1890s.

was Town Clerk, and he very kindly gave me facilities for my study. First of all, this being in 1890 or 1891, I wrote a history of Coventry for a prize offered by Mrs Humphrey Ward for a history of a town. I did not get it. In fact I never do win prizes. I always come out second, as I did in this case, the winner being Miss Alice Greenwood, who wrote "The Hanoverian Queens". Mrs J.R. Green, widow of the historian, read my article and suggested that I try to elaborate it for the Press because a great deal of the information was obtained from old manuscripts which had never been published...

... I took the advice of Mrs Green and part of the essay was published in the 'English Historical Review' in 1894."

That MDH was able to teach herself to read mediaeval manuscripts says much for her dedication and scholarship. In those times at the end of the nineteenth century few people had the necessary background knowledge to enable them to do the work today done by trained archivists. The knowledge she had previously acquired of Early English, Latin, French and German stood her in very good stead and she soon became more experienced than most.

An amusing story is told of her labours in the Treasury in St Mary's Hall for she once became locked in at the end of the day. The caretaker suddenly realized that she might not have left, and he went back to check. It is said that she had been so engrossed in her work that she had been unaware of her plight.

STAYING AT DIAL HOUSE, ASHOW, WITH THE DORMERS

The 1891 Census revealed that Mrs Harris was living with her brother James, his second wife and their four young children at Dial House Farm and that MDH was also living there at that time. Described as a governess, she may have been conducting spells of research in Coventry, which was only seven miles away, or she may have been on holiday from a post in London. As John Garner Dormer, the twenty-four year old son of James Dormer's first marriage, was also living in the house, as were two female servants, the place must have been somewhat crowded.

NUMBER 2, DALMENY AVENUE, ISLINGTON

The Association of Old Students of Lady Margaret Hall was founded in 1892 and in the first few annual reports the address of MDH is given as 2 Dalmeny Avenue, Camden Road, NW, which is close to the rear of Holloway Prison.

It would seem highly likely that for a number of years, MDH had stayed very frequently at this address and when she was teaching in Kensington, she may have travelled daily. Her second cousin Mary Savage (usually known as Dolly) was nine years younger, but it must have been pleasant for MDH to have some young company and be a part of the Savage household. I do not know for how long Thomas Savage was a Professor of Mathematics, but MDH probably relished discussing important matters with him and his wife. Some letters still exist which were written by Dolly Savage to her parents from Brittany, where she went for a holiday in the

THE FOUR CHILDREN IN THIS PHOTOGRAPH (TAKEN IN 1895) WERE COUSINS OF MARY DORMER HARRIS. Margaret Elizabeth Dormer (right) was aged 11, James Garrard 10, Elin Mary 8 and Sara Phyllis (left) was 7. They were the children of James Alfred Dormer and his second wife, Ellen Elizabeth. It would appear that MDH's mother lived with this family at the Dial House Farm, Ashow, for long periods between 1890 and 1895.

mid 1890s. Knowing that MDH was close to the family, it seems more than likely that she accompanied Dolly on her travels.

In the 1890s Dalmeny Avenue was a quiet road, with a mixture of reasonably large houses, suitable for middle-class families. The area was close to several main railway stations and places of interest, and because of this useful position there were many lodgers amongst the inhabitants.

Although I have not visited there myself, I understand that Dalmeny Avenue is quite different today. Many of the houses were destroyed in the Second World War and have since been rebuilt as flats. This would appear to be the case with Number 2.

LETTER TO JAMES MURRAY

It is clear that MDH worked for a time on the Oxford English Dictionary with James A.H. Murray in Oxford. A letter by MDH written from Dalmeny Avenue, dated December 11th 1894, to James Murray in Oxford, is preserved amongst the

AS A YOUNG WOMAN, MARY DORMER HARRIS OFTEN STAYED WITH A COUSIN MARY SAVAGE AND HER FAMILY IN DALMENY AVENUE, ISLINGTON, IN NORTH LONDON. This photograph of Dalmeny Avenue, taken about 1895, shows a mixture of houses suitable for relatively wealthy, middle-class families.

archives of the Oxford University Press. In the letter MDH states that she will be with James Murray at one o'clock tomorrow and that she will be very pleased to accept his kind invitation to lunch.

James Murray, together with his wife Ada and numerous children, lived in a house named "Sunnyside" in the Banbury Road in Oxford. He had moved there especially to complete the Oxford English Dictionary, for it had been planned for many years and was proving to be a far greater undertaking than had previously been thought. A Scriptorium had been built in the garden, but this was little better than a tin-roofed shed. It was sunk a few feet into the ground because the professor who lived next door had complained that its construction would spoil his view.

THE SCRIPTORIUM

James Murray was apparently very fussy concerning his assistants for he had been working as Editor for many years on the dictionary. His standards were

IN 1895 MDH WENT TO OXFORD TO ACT AS ONE OF THE ASSISTANTS TO JAMES MURRAY, THEN COMPILING THE OXFORD ENGLISH DICTIONARY. This photograph shows the complete Murray family with all eleven children, and when she worked in the Scriptorium in the garden of their home, "Sunnyside" 78 Banbury Road, Oxford, MDH would have seen much of the younger children.

extremely high and one can only suppose that after he had entertained MDH to lunch and found her enthusiastic and full of common sense, he decided to ask her to join his staff. Her working day in the Scriptorium was probably spent collating the slips of paper on which the definitions were written or perhaps checking words or quotations.

The Scriptorium was said to be hot in summer and cold and damp in winter, but MDH suffered the conditions and worked with James Murray for maybe a year or more. In the Supplement to the Dictionary which appeared in 1932, her name appears amongst the names of the official assistants.

A delightful story is told of the younger Murray children and the Scriptorium in "Caught in the Web of Words", a biography of James Murray written by his granddaughter K. M. Elisabeth Murray in 1977. Although he was a strict disciplinarian and expected his children to help by sometimes sorting slips for the dictionary, James Murray was also charismatic and very kind. His children were equally fun-loving and hard-working. Sometimes when James Murray went out in

THIS FAMOUS PHOTOGRAPH OF JAMES A. H. MURRAY IN THE SCRIPTORIUM SHOWS HOW THOUSANDS OF SLIPS FOR THE DICTIONARY WERE SORTED, BUNDLED AND STORED. Mary Dormer Harris worked in the Scriptorium alongside Murray and others.

the summer, his younger children would venture into the garden and play "German Bands" which meant blowing down the spouts of the numerous watering-cans which were always at hand. Often one of the assistants would then come out of the Scriptorium and give the children a penny to go away. I like to think that MDH took part in this exercise for later in life she often used to do the same thing to beggars when they knocked on her door in Leamington Spa.

DR JOSEPH WRIGHT

James Murray was not the only man in Oxford who was working on a dictionary because Joseph Wright was working on a Dialect Dictionary.

Whilst the Brown Book of the Old Students Association of her Oxford college did not mention that she was helping James Murray, that same book did mention the fact that MDH was helping Joseph Wright with his dictionary. The report for 1894-95 stated that she was at work at the Oxford University Press, under Dr Wright and certainly the name of MDH appears as a Voluntary Reader in the Introduction to the English Dialect Dictionary which was re-printed in 1961, after initially being published in instalments between 1896 and 1905. MDH is also listed as one of the

JOSEPH WRIGHT EDITED THE ENGLISH DIALECT DICTIONARY AND WAS A GREAT FRIEND OF JAMES MURRAY IN OXFORD. Mary Dormer Harris assisted Wright at the Oxford University Press for a time in the mid 1890s before the Dialect Dictionary appeared in instalments between 1896 and 1905.

Correspondents of the dictionary, but this was obviously slightly later in life for her address is given as Leamington.

To help with one dictionary seems like a great deal of hard work but to be listed as a helper on two major works of reference seems to single her out as a widely-read, reliable scholar. It may have been that there were few trained workers who had the necessary expertise to be able to help with difficult quotations, especially from very early works in English.

NEEDED IN LEAMINGTON in 1896

Mrs Harris perhaps continued to live at Dial House Farm with her brother James and his family for several years, but eventually it seems that she decided to live independently in Leamington. A kinsman John Dormer had taken over the farm, but with so many family members of around the same age sharing the same name and initials, it is not entirely clear whether it was her nephew John Garner Dormer or not.

In 1896 it was thought best if MDH, then twenty-nine, left Oxford and returned home to Warwickshire to live with her mother. As Florence Hayllar put it many years later *"since her widowed mother needed her...she settled down in Leamington."* With plenty of contacts in the academic world, MDH may have given up the prospect of a promising career in Oxford, but she never complained, and at least the move provided her with spare time in which to write.

9 SHERBOURNE TERRACE (CLARENDON STREET) LEAMINGTON SPA WAS THE HOME OF MARY DORMER HARRIS AND HER MOTHER FOR AROUND TEN YEARS FROM 1896 TO 1905.

MDH's move back to mid-Warwickshire must have been in late 1896 or early 1897, for the first mention of her in the local street directories was in 1897. Mother and daughter were then living at 9 Sherbourne Terrace, a medium-sized house in Clarendon Street, in Leamington Spa.

Almost certainly Mrs and Miss Harris had a female servant for such domestic help was cheap and those who could afford to pay wages were expected to provide employment for the poor. With very few benefits available to the needy, a lowly paid, menial domestic position offered to a teenage girl often meant a great deal to a large working-class family. Furthermore, if middle-class social contacts were to be maintained, she and her mother had to observe the rules dictated by those class-conscious times.

MDH considered Leamington to be a good centre for her work as there were good road and rail links and the house they had chosen was in a pleasant area of the town. The rooms were probably furnished with items from Dale House.

PAPERS FOR ANTIQUARIAN SOCIETIES. FIRST BOOK ON COVENTRY 1898

After some correspondence with Mrs Green, the widow of the historian T.R. Green, who advised her to experiment and try for publication in several ways, MDH made a number of contacts.

In 1894 part of her original essay on the history of Coventry had been published by the 'English Historical Review' and in 1895 she wrote a paper on the "Craft Guilds of Coventry" for the Society of Antiquaries. However that society did not admit women so a man read the paper for her on November 21st 1895 and she was not even allowed to be present while it was being read. It may have been the Honorary Secretary, Hercules Read, or the Assistant Secretary, St John Hope, who read the paper, which was a typical, detailed piece of work from MDH, containing many references to the Coventry Leet Book.

(I am indebted to the Society of Antiquaries of London for information and a copy of the proceedings at which this paper was read.)

In 1898 MDH's first book was published. Entitled "Life in An Old English Town," it described the history of Coventry in some detail. The book was part of the Social England series and the publishers were Swan Sonnenschein & Co. While living in Oxford, MDH had become friendly with the well-known writer and academic Lucy Toulmin Smith, and this busy woman actually helped to correct the proofs of the book.

Reviews of the book were very favourable and initial sales were good, but as is so often the case, future sales did not match this first optimistic run. The publishers decided not to reprint and MDH became somewhat discouraged.

LETTERS FROM WELL KNOWN PEOPLE

In mid 2001 I was delighted to learn from Nancy Dormer Gutch, a second cousin of Mary Dormer Harris, that a number of letters sent to her during this period have been preserved. It would appear that when her book on Coventry appeared, MDH sent copies to several well-known writers and historians who had helped her or whom she felt would appreciate her work.

One reply from the Rev Augustus Jessop thanked her for the copy of her book and a similar letter came from Samuel Rawson Gardiner. Both were highly-respected historians of the time. Perhaps the most famous of the writers who sent letters of thanks to her was Walter Besant, author of many novels, social histories and books on London.

It was probably after she had became discouraged by low sales that, at the suggestion of her mother, MDH wrote to Scottish writer Jane Findlater, who wrote back in an undated letter,

"I can't agree with you that writing books is a cheerless affair, for to me it is the great joy and support of life; but I must admit that it is attended by many discouragements. One often doubts whether one's work has any value and even, in moments of depression, whether it is worth doing at all. Then kind and appreciative letters like yours come in and cheer one on."

A LECTURER AND HISTORIAN

Little by little, despite the fact that she was a female in a male-dominated field, MDH began to carve out for herself a historical career and she became well-known in the Midlands as a lecturer and writer. At no stage did she appear to contemplate marriage for that would have effectively ended her professional career.

In 1899 MDH wrote another paper for a historical association, but this time she was allowed to read the paper herself. On December 13th 1899 she read her paper "The Manuscript Records of Coventry" to the Birmingham and Warwickshire Archaeological Society. It would appear that she was the first woman to do this, although Lucy Toulmin Smith had had a paper read for her some years before.

From this time onwards MDH had many connections with the Birmingham Archaeological Society and some years later she read other papers to them. "The Mediaeval Shoes found at Coventry" and "Misericords of Coventry" were both read and later printed in the Journal of the Society.

THE LEET BOOK IS BEGUN

1900 saw the thirty-three year old Mary Dormer Harris continuing her career as a serious writer and lecturer. Living mostly with her mother in Leamington Spa, she was sometimes able to take holidays abroad, just as she had when she had been a teenager.

In 1904 the greatest work of her life was started, perhaps rather reluctantly. The mediaeval Coventry Leet Book had never been properly transcribed and she invited the extremely well-known Frederick Furnivall to come from Oxford to appraise the volume, with a view to publication by the Early English Text Society. However Dr Furnivall, who was probably familiar with MDH's work on the dictionaries with

James Murray and Joseph Wright, persuaded her to undertake the work herself.

MDH wrote of Dr Furnivall,

"Upon my suggestion he came down to Coventry and saw the Leet Book which he asked me to copy as it stood. I agreed and the City Council, for my convenience, allowed the Leet Book to be deposited in the Leamington Free Library, where I did my work. That was in 1904 so the work on and off occupied ten years. At the beginning I found the work very difficult and I was much discouraged."

It was a huge undertaking for anyone, let alone a single woman with family commitments and few, if any, other scholars close at hand with whom she could discuss difficult questions concerning Latin, Norman-French or Early English.

THE FORMER PUBLIC LIBRARY IN LEAMINGTON WHERE, FOR ALMOST TEN YEARS FROM 1903 TO 1912, MARY DORMER HARRIS WORKED ON HER TRANSCRIPTION OF THE COVENTRY LEET BOOK. This photograph shows the library as it was when she was a frequent visitor there.

INSERT: DR FREDERICK FURNIVALL ENCOURAGED MARY DORMER HARRIS TO TRANSCRIBE THE COVENTRY LEET BOOK FOR THE EARLY ENGLISH TEXT SOCIETY. He was an extremely energetic man with a forceful, yet many say charismatic, personality.

4. MOVING HOUSE, SUFFRAGISTS AND BOOKS 1906 -1913

16 GAVESTON ROAD 1906

Sometime at the end of 1905 Mary Dormer Harris and her mother decided to move house. New houses were being built at Milverton, near St Mark's Church in the Rugby Road in Leamington and they decided that a new start in a pleasant area would suit them well. As MDH needed to travel to Coventry quite frequently, the new house was only a few minutes walk away from Milverton Station where there was a regular service of trains to Coventry on the LNWR (later LMS) line.

Local directories of 1906 show that they had already moved into number 16 and that they were amongst the first residents of Gaveston Road. The odd numbered houses were still under construction.

At that time the population of Leamington was far less than it is now, being less than twenty seven thousand in 1901. Many of the households in newly-built Gaveston Road would have had a part-time maid, as MDH and her mother appear to have done.

The three-bedroomed, terraced houses in Gaveston Road were typically Edwardian, well-built of brick, with fair-sized rooms, including a bathroom. With

16 GAVESTON ROAD IN LEAMINGTON SPA WAS THE HOME OF MARY DORMER HARRIS FOR AROUND THIRTY YEARS.

three rooms downstairs, plus a scullery and larder, they would have been easy to run. A small but adequate back garden, with access to a back lane through a garden gate, enabled later occupants to build a garage close to the house.

THE SUFFRAGE MOVEMENT

Throughout the early years of the twentieth century, MDH did what she could to help the cause of women's suffrage and her name occasionally crops up in reports of meetings in the local papers.

In 1898 there was the first mention of the National Union of Women's Suffrage Societies (NUWSS) in Leamington and it was to this moderate group known as Suffragists that MDH gave her support. In other areas more militant groups, such as the Women's Social and Political Union (WSPU) led by the Pankhursts, were active and they were known as Suffragettes.

In 1905 the first meeting of the Leamington & Warwick Women's Suffrage Society was held, but no details were reported in the newspapers. However the second meeting on 20th March 1906 was reported in the Leamington Spa Courier of March 23rd.

The meeting, held in the Masonic Rooms and reasonably well-attended, was presided over by Mrs Bassett of Birmingham. Miss Vellacott, the Secretary, read her report and Mrs Dykes as Treasurer gave her financial report. When it was proposed that the reports be adopted, then printed and circulated, MDH seconded the motion.

MRS ELLEN DYKES (1859-1937)

Mrs Dykes was eight years older than MDH, with a husband and three grown-up children, but she was a tireless worker for a variety of worthwhile causes in the early decades of the twentieth century. She was a County Councillor for 18 years and also a JP. In 1920 she was awarded the OBE and in 1921, after the death of her husband she and several members of her family moved to 22 Gaveston Road, just three doors away from MDH.

However to return to the days when the Suffragists were still fighting hard for their cause, Mrs Dykes and MDH must have grown to know each other quite well. Their circumstances and lives were vastly different, but from 1905 onwards, both added common-sense and dignity to the feminist cause.

LETTERS FROM CHRISTABEL PANKHURST

Amongst the collection of letters sent to MDH and still preserved by her family, are two from Christabel Pankhurst, the daughter of Emmeline Pankhurst, founder of the WSPU and the leader of the militant suffragettes. Writing from 60 Upper Brook Street, Manchester on 5th April 1906 Christabel Pankhurst said,

"Dear Miss Dormer Harris,

You spoke so kindly and approvingly of the work which the Women's Social and Political Union is doing that I am going to ask you to help us. What I mean is that

ALDERMAN ELLEN DYKES, OBE, JP, (1859-1937) WAS AN ASSOCIATE OF MARY DORMER HARRIS FOR MANY YEARS. They were fellow suffragists in the early years of the twentieth century and in 1921 Mrs Dykes and her family moved to 22 Gaveston Road, only three doors away from MDH and her mother.

I think you must know women suffragists in your part of the world who would be willing to subscribe to our funds. Our members are nearly all working women and they cannot give much money though they give as much as ever they can. It would touch you to see what sacrifices they make."

After outlining various activities in London which had all cost money, Christabel Pankhurst went on,

"We are full of big schemes. Is it too much to ask you I wonder to get any of your friends who approve of our work to help us with money? Subscriptions could be sent to to Mrs Dean, Hon Sec. Women's Social and Political Union, 6 Gerald Road, Lower Broughton, Manchester.

I must tell you that Mr Winston Churchill has said to members of the National Liberal Club who predicted that we should soon get tired of the agitation, that we should never get tired — to this he added the statement that we are dreadful women, so persistent."

I do not know if MDH sent any money to the funds of the WSPU, but I like to think that she did for a note from Christabel Pankhurst, dated 5th July 1906, was written from 45, Park Walk, Chelsea.

"Many thanks for congratulations. I shall almost certainly be in Birmingham soon, but I will let you know later.

Today I saw the ? who are in Holloway. They are very firm. My sister is in prison..." Nancy Dormer Gutch tells me that family tradition has it that MDH once chained herself to some railings. Although there is no official mention of this and MDH belonged to the non-militant suffragist organisation, most certainly she showed some sympathy with the Pankhursts in the early days.

Also in 1906 MDH had written to Bernard Shaw, a man she much admired, asking him to make public statements in favour of the women's suffrage movement. He declined saying,

"I have done so much campaigning on the subject in the past that my views are somewhat stale, not to mention that I have a reputation for singular and extreme opinions and it is very desirable that Women's rights should not be associated with anything out of the normal common sense run.

Thank you all the same for the suggestion.

Yours faithfully,

G. Bernard Shaw"

THE SUFFRAGE PROCESSION IN LONDON

Together with the letters to MDH was an article reprinted from the "Leamington Chronicle" of Feb. 15th 1907 which described *"The Suffrage Procession by a Processionist."*

This article could well have been written by MDH for it seems likely that she took part in the procession and it is a highly-competent piece of journalism. At the end, the article tried to assess the usefulness of the march.

"Did we touch London? Perhaps. A picture teaches a child far better than the written word and men and women, who are mostly grown-up children, would get a more vivid notion of the actuality of the suffrage movement from seeing thousands of actual suffragists tramp the streets than from reading the most lucid statements in newspapers. Action is sometimes better than argument in a cause like ours."

THE VICTORIA COUNTY HISTORY OF WARWICKSHIRE

In 1908 Volume Two of the Victoria County History of Warwickshire was published and pages 137 to 182 carried a section on "Social and Economic History" written by MDH.

The title of the entry in this most prestigious of history series sounds somewhat daunting, but MDH packed the pages with a mass of interesting details of people such as highwaymen John Smith and his faithful love Elizabeth Beere.

"The former, one of the notorious Culworth gang, was hanged in 1788 at Warwick for a highway robbery at Gaydon, and Elizabeth, having witnessed the hanging, bore the body away that night on a donkey and panniers to Culworth for burial."

On the same page we learn that following improvements to the roads, made possible by the work of Telford and Macadam, the Tally-ho coach ran from London to Birmingham on May Day 1830 in seven and half hours, and later in the section we have the stirring tale of Laurence Saunders in Coventry.

"The struggle in Coventry for the preservation of grazing rights brings to light the interesting personality of Laurence Saunders, who for some sixteen years (1480-96) was a thorn in the sides of the fathers of the city. Year after year he protested against surcharging and inclosures. Twice he was put in prison, and if he came again for the third time, he was told, 'it should cost him his head.' It probably did cost him his life; Henry VII made a Star Chamber matter of the business, and Laurence vanished into the Fleet Prison in 1496, and is heard of no more. But he had a great following in the city..."

This last is a fine example of a cross-over of MDH's work for at the same time as she was writing the entry for the Victoria County History, she was continuing the first transcription of the Coventry Leet Book, which contains the details of Saunders.

THE PLACE OF WOMEN

Always bearing in mind the idea that votes for women were just around the corner and that the lot of women generally needed to be improved, MDH did what most male historians did not do and that was mention the lot of women in history.

She had very harsh words concerning the employment of women who were forced to spin in the fifteenth century in Coventry, *"...Indeed, spinners were notoriously oppressed and cheated by their employers..."* MDH then went on to condemn modern employers in 1908 and she wrote passionately of the oppressed factory girls in Birmingham.

"...One other section of the Warwickshire industrial world is still unorganised, namely the Birmingham women home workers, some of whom are the worst-paid recruits of the great army of labour. The earnings of the hook and eye carders have made this occupation a byword for sweating, while the average wage of the women factory hand is but 10sh to 10sh. 6d a week."

A footnote by MDH quotes another book which said that *"the hook and eye carders earn an average of 3sh. 3½d. a week"* and I imagine that the factory owners in Birmingham loved her for mentioning that!

Later MDH outlined how the lot of women seemed to have grown more restricted since Mediaeval times.

"Women occupied an important position in mediaeval town life; they were members of gilds, partook of feasts, and in the election of gild officers."

That last remark was surely intended to be noticed by those against the suffrage cause currently being waged by MDH and many women throughout Britain.

MDH also included the wills of two Warwickshire widows of the Middle Ages, first Joan, Lady Bergavenny (will dated 10 January 1434-5) and then Mistress Johan Hungerford, formerly widow of Edmund Lucy of Charlecote (will proved 5th August 1514). The list of clothes and linen belonging to Lady Bergavenny is particularly interesting for there is a delightful portrait of her in the Aylesford Collection in Birmingham Archives and some years later, MDH included a black and white print of this as an illustration in her transcription of the Trinity Guild Register.

THE COVENTRY LEET BOOK

Throughout the whole of the period 1904 to 1913 the matter of the transcription, editing and publication of the Coventry Leet Book was an on-going process. MDH fitted in the work when she could and she became a very frequent visitor to Leamington Reference Library where the manuscript book was housed.

At this time MDH was aged around forty, and for the first time that is known, her eyesight began to cause problems. Short-sighted from her youth, she began to suffer considerable eye-strain as she endeavoured to decipher almost illegible passages. Afterwards her friends said that she had irreparably damaged her sight, but she herself never complained.

The Leet Book was published in four sections between 1907 and 1913 and I think the EDITOR'S PREFACE by MDH at the commencement of the last volume summarizes both her own difficulties and the specialist help she received from other scholars when checking the proofs.

"Now that my laborious task is ended I have only to thank those who made its accomplishment possible by so generously giving their time to inform my ignorance, correct my faulty Latin and Anglo-French and suggest textual emendations."

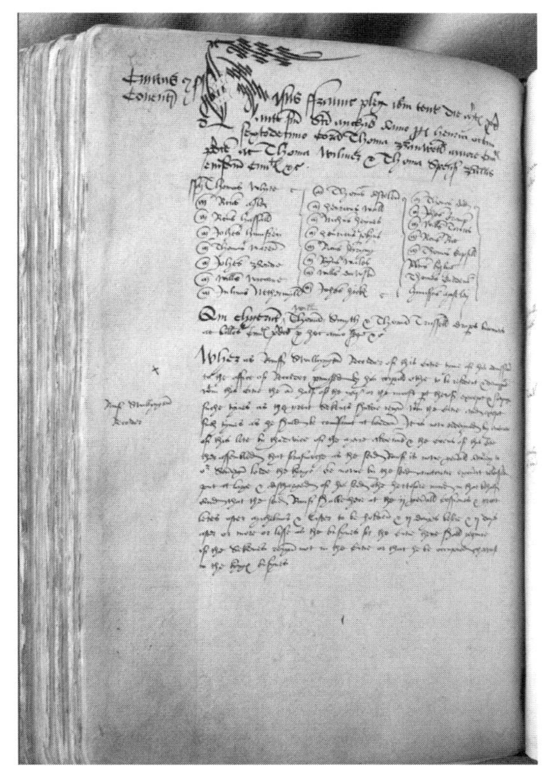

A PAGE FROM THE COVENTRY LEET BOOK. There are 436 numbered pages in the book (plus a few unnumbered leaves) and most of the content concerns mayoral elections and court sittings in Coventry betwen 1421 and 1555.

MDH went on to thank W.H. Stevenson, the late R.E.G. Kirk and his son E.F.Kirk, Dr H. Bradley, G.J. Turner, William Page, S.O. Addy, George Buchanan and the late Miss Toulmin Smith. All were respected highly scholars and writers of the time. MDH ended with a great compliment to the late Dr Frederick Furnivall, a charismatic and influential figure in the late 19th and early twentieth century.

The last sentence in the EDITOR'S PREFACE in which MDH thanks Miss Jessie Hayllar for compiling *"The full and careful name-index of this volume"* gives us an interesting personal reference for Jessie Hayllar was the sister of Florence Hayllar, MDH's great friend whom she had met at Lady Margaret Hall, over twenty years previously.

DESCRIPTION OF THE LEET BOOK

In early March 2001 I was privileged to be shown the Leet Book in Coventry Archive Office and the photographs contained in this book will give readers some idea of its impressive size and appearance. For a description of the book however, I cannot do better than quote that given by MDH in a footnote in her first section (page xi) of her Introduction.

THE COVENTRY LEET BOOK IS A MASSIVE VOLUME, WITH COVERS MEASURING 16½ INCHES BY 11½ INCHES. It is nearly five inches thick and there are remains of clasps.

"The covers measure 16½ in. x 11½ in. and the book is 4 and three quarters in. thick from cover to cover. There are remains of clasps and the leather bears impressions of seals with the Lamb and the legend "Ecce Agnus Dei".

...The great bulk of this volume ...is occupied by the record of mayoral elections and court sittings between 1421 and 1555"

For the vast majority of us the Leet Book makes difficult reading, even in transcription, but to mediaeval scholars the world over it is a storehouse of information. Few towns or cities possess such an ancient volume and at the time when the Leet Book was written, Coventry was one of the most important cities in England.

"THE STORY OF COVENTRY" PUBLISHED IN 1911

In 1911 MDH's most popular book on Coventry appeared as one in a series of histories of mediaeval towns. In part it was a revamp of the book of 1898, but published by a different company, in a small hardback volume with plenty of illustrations by the very able Albert Chanler.

MDH's Introductory Chapter "The Three Spires and Coventry" contains numerous fine-sounding sentences which are as true today as the day she wrote

"THE THREE SPIRES REMAIN YET AND GIVE GREETING TO ALL THOSE WHO APPROACH COVENTRY." So wrote Mary Dormer Harris in 1911 and her words are just as true today, over ninety years later. The spire on the left is that of Holy Trinity Church, whilst that in the middle is that of St Michael's, the Cathedral from 1918. The Quadrant, where Angela, Amy and Dr Walter Brazil resided, is immediately below Christchurch, which is the spire to the right.

them. After quoting lines from Drayton's "Polyolbion" in which he refers to the spires as "proud pyramidès" she said,

"But the 'proud pyramidès,' the 'three spires' remain yet, and give greeting to all those who approach Coventry, dominating the flat midland country for many a mile, changing their relative position as the spectator moves, and their colour in the shifting lights."

A little further on in the introductory chapter MDH wrote of Coventry,

"It is a typically English city, whose history might serve as the "abstract and brief chronicle" of England."

and later,

"In the country round about Coventry two Englands meet, one a land of green woods and well-watered pastures, the other black with the toil of the coal fields."

Like many people, every time I travel on a bus to Coventry, I am fascinated by views of the three spires, so aptly described by MDH over ninety years ago. As for MDH's green woods, when I first travelled to Coventry from Leamington at bluebell time, I was amazed and delighted to see the wonderful patches of ancient-looking woods, within a mile or so of the city centre.

THIS DRAWING OF THE MINSTREL GALLERY IN ST MARY'S HALL WAS ONE OF ALBERT CHANLER'S ILLUSTRATIONS FOR MARY DORMER HARRIS'S BOOK "THE STORY OF COVENTRY" PUBLISHED IN 1911. In after years she made many speeches in this fine mediaeval hall.

GODIVA AND COVENTRY

In a chapter entitled "Leofric and Godiva" MDH explores many aspects of history and also folk lore.

"Godiva is traditionally represented riding on a white horse. It is curious that an illuminated document formerly in the possesion of the Smiths' company, two Godivas appear, one as a white woman on a white horse and another a black woman on an elephant - the last in allusion to the elephant and castle, the arms of the city."

Footnotes are sometimes merely boring references, but the footnote to this remark tells quite a story.

"Coventry Standard, Jan 15-16, 1909. The MS (1684 -1833) has passed into private hands, and I have never been able to see it."

I would cite these few remarks as being typical of MDH's extreme thoroughness in that she often thought of those scholars who would come after her. After many speculations and references to Godiva and her horse, she brings us straight back to hard fact.

"For many people Coventry suggests Godiva. It is always well to bear in mind she was an authentic person, wife of Leofric, mother of Aelfgar, Earl of East Anglia... grandmother of the Earls Edwin and Morkere, and of Aldgyth, first wife, then widow, of Gruffydd, Prince of Wales; then wife and widow of Harold, King of England."

OTHER WOMEN IN COVENTRY'S HISTORY

Once again MDH did what she did in her other books and she included a short section about women in Coventry's history in "The Story of Coventry."

"Women have always been to the fore in Coventry; the names rise of S. Osburg, Godiva, Isabella, Margaret of Anjou, of the virgin sisters Botoner, who built the spire (of St Michael's) and of Joan Ward, the first Coventry Lollard martyr. Women of the city, too, helped to keep out Charles 1. Here Sarah Kemble, (Mrs Siddons) was married and Miss Ellen Terry born. It is fitting that the chief literary interest of Coventry should centre on a woman's name. George Eliot went to school at a house in the south-west end of Warwick Row, 1832 -5. Coventry is said to be the original of Middlemarch, and S. Mary's Hall is described in the trial scene of "Adam Bede".

A LETTER FROM LUCY TOULMIN SMITH

From one extant letter to MDH we learn that she must have known the scholarly Lucy Toulmin Smith, the first woman in England to be appointed Head of a Public Library, quite well. In 1894 Miss Toulmin Smith had left Highgate in London, where she had lived for many years with her father, to take up her post as Librarian of Manchester College, Oxford. Very soon her house was known as a meeting place for young people and doubtless MDH had visited her many times when living in Oxford. The letter from 1 Park Terrace, Oxford, had been written on April 28th, only a few months before Lucy Toulmin Smith's death at the end of 1911.

The main part of the letter concerns matters about St Michael, the descent into Hell and Mystery Plays, but in the additional information comes much of interest, from one scholar and author to another.

Miss Toulmin Smith says she is sorry that MDH has been worried with law trouble *"T'is quite tiresome."* What this trouble was we have no idea.

The letter ends,

"My love to you and your Mother,
Yours affectionately,
L. Toulmin Smith"

There is also a fascinating post script, hastily scribbled above the address on the first page, which tells us that then as now, writers found it difficult to get their work published in the way they wanted.

"Do you find Dent a fair man to deal with? I've been thinking of trying him for something, but several friends rather put me off him." Dent had of course just published MDH's book "The Story of Coventry".

1913 WAS A DIFFICULT YEAR FOR SUFFRAGISTS

1913 was a very active year as regards the cause of women's suffrage and in early July Lady Willoughby de Broke held an "At Home" at Compton Verney in connection with the the Conservative and Unionist Women's Franchise Association. The event was fully reported in the "Warwick Advertiser" of Saturday July 12th 1913 and MDH was listed as being one of the two hundred or so guests from all over Warwickshire who attended the meeting. Miss Lea, Headmistress of the King's High School for Girls in Warwick, also attended, as did Miss Ahrons, the Second Mistress.

First Lady Willoughby de Broke received the visitors on the lawn in front of the house, then speeches were held in the Great Yard. Tea was served on small tables on a grass plot surrounded by lime trees and after the meeting the ground-floor rooms of Compton Verney were thrown open for those who wished to look around. It was reported that her ladyship's footmen wore the colours of the CUWFA.

However the following week, July 19th 1913, the Warwick Advertiser reported a vastly different kind of suffrage meeting.

"THE PILGRIMS" 1913

In the summer of 1913 the "Pilgrims" of the non-militant suffrage societies organised a nation-wide march and travellers from the north of England arrived in Warwick on Tuesday 15th July. There was an open-air meeting in the Market Place and Lady Willoughby de Broke and others spoke at an orderly afternoon meeting. Later a procession formed up, headed by the Leamington Spa Band, and the Suffragists marched to Leamington.

ALTHOUGH SHE WAS A SUFFRAGIST AND BELONGED TO A NON-MILITANT SUFFRAGE SOCIETY, MARY DORMER HARRIS HAD MUCH SYMPATHY WITH THE MORE MILITANT SUFFRAGETTES, LED BY MRS PANKHURST. In this photograph, probably taken in 1913, Suffragettes and their supporters are marching through Stratford-upon- Avon.

Although MDH's mother was nearly eighty years old, she turned out to wave to the women and could be clearly seen on the edge of the pavement. MDH, at the age of forty-five, was almost certainly one of the marchers.

In contrast to the meeting in Warwick, once the marchers had arrived in the Parade in Leamington, the event became extremely rowdy. The Warwick Advertiser's headline ran, *"Exciting Scenes at Leamington."*

At the Obelisk near Leamington Town Hall, the crowd was too large for one speaker to be heard, so six improvised platforms were erected. All the speakers were frequently interrupted and there was occasionally some disorder in the crowd. It may well have been that MDH, as an experienced public speaker, gave one of the impromptu talks.

After the meeting the Pilgrims made their way to the Liberal CLub where their luggage was stored. While they were there an unruly crowd gathered outside and the police *"were subject to a good deal of annoyance, turf, tomatoes and other things being thrown about."* The Pilgrims left peaceably, only by being helped by nearby residents and using the gardens of adjoining houses to make their escape.

The large crowds in the Parade however were slow to disperse and suddenly around 9.20 p.m. there was a *"hoofing and yelling, and looking up the Parade one saw a dense crowd racing along. We regret to state that the hooligans, joined by the riff-raff and many a strong man, chased a suffragist round into Regent Street."*

The unfortunate woman turned out to be Miss Sharpe of Birmingham, Secretary of the Leamington Branch of the NUWSS, who was making her way to Clarendon Street. When set upon by *"some irresponsible roughs"* she had to take refuge in the doorway of an empty shop in Regent Street. Mr Quaintance, a member of the Men's League (supporters of Women's suffrage) and the Police came to her aid and eventually she was escorted to Clarendon Street.

It was highly likely that during this rowdy meeting and its aftermath that MDH was very close to the action for she, along with around twenty other women and a couple of men, were listed as Official Stewards for the event.

AN UNSETTLED WORLD IN 1913

Not only was the world moving towards war in 1914 but many things were changing. Not long after MDH's book on Coventry appeared in 1911, there was a great threat to the old mediaeval streets she had described so eloquently and she and others wondered how to stop it. The problem was that some people began to feel that the ancient centre of the city of Coventry was inappropriate for modern life. The

BUTCHER ROW IN COVENTRY CONTAINED SOME FINE MEDIAEVAL BUILDINGS AND WAS AN EXTREMELY PICTURESQUE STREET. This is how MDH first saw it in the late nineteenth century.

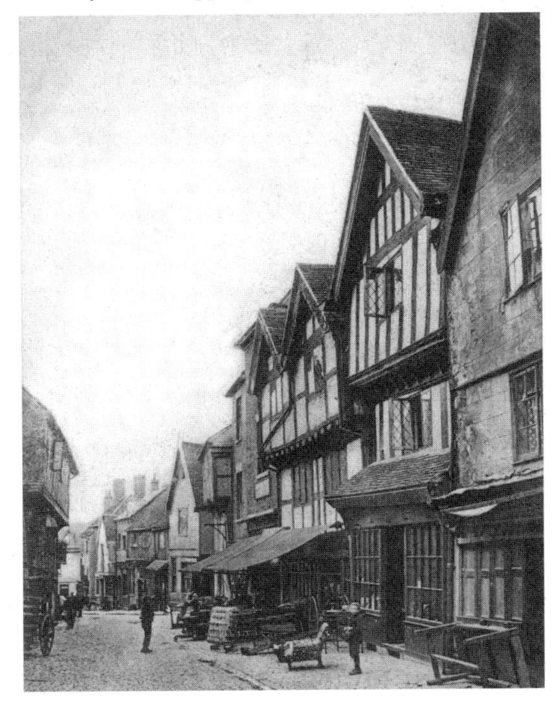

quaint and narrow streets such as Little Butcher Row, where many shops and houses had overhanging upper storeys, were felt to be incompatible with the new growth in motorized traffic. Some members of the Corporation of Coventry began to contemplate demolishing whole areas in the heart of the city and building wide through roads, together with modern retail and industrial premises.

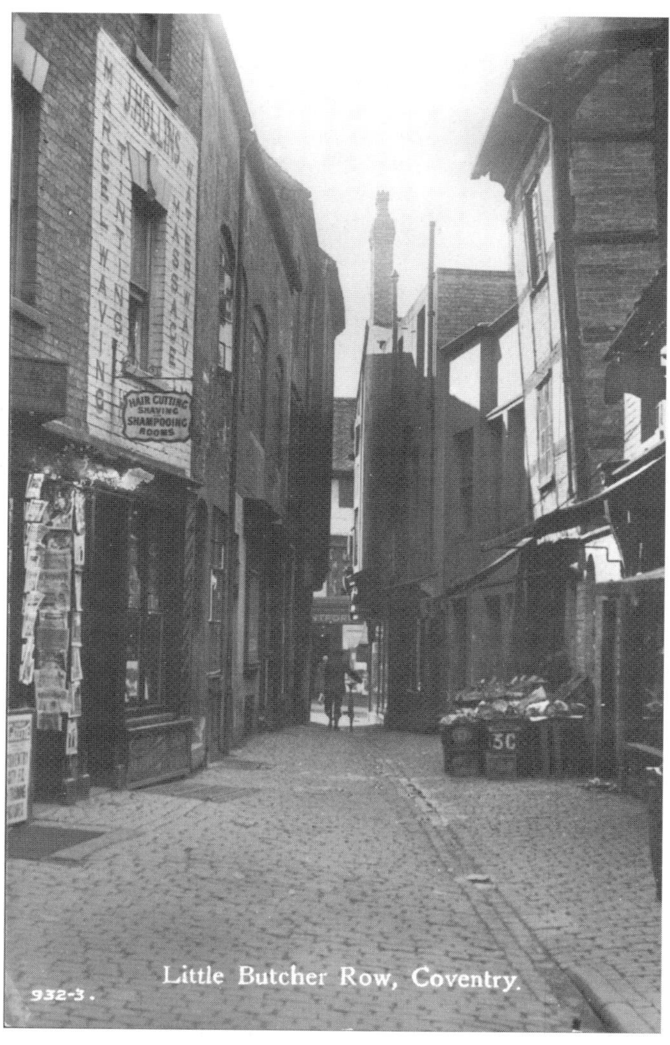

LITTLE BUTCHER ROW, AS PHOTOGRAPHED FROM BUTCHER ROW AROUND 1912. It was to try to save mediaeval streets such as this that the Coventry City Guild was formed in 1914.

5. THE FIRST WORLD WAR AND PRIVATE BATTLES 1914 - 1923

THE FIRST WORLD WAR

Years later Mary Dormer Harris explained to a young friend that in 1914 when they read in the newspapers that the Grand Duke Ferdinand had been assassinated, they did not know it meant war. With no radio or television programmes to provide instant information, the complexities of foreign events were sometimes unclear. She explained,

"You can't remember 1914. I can. When the murder at Sarajevo happened no one had any idea the fires were lit all over the world."

As a sincere liberal thinker, committed to making the world a better and fairer place for all, throughout her life MDH did all she could to help the cause of world peace. As a historian she realised that shows of force and cruel acts had never solved any of the major problems in the past and that what was really important was dialogue and a greater understanding of all peoples and their problems. Like many of her fellow suffragists she reasoned that world rulers were almost always men, and men in general were more inclined to opt for war to solve the world's difficulties. Therefore it was desirous, not only for women to have the vote, but also for them to serve on Councils and in National Parliaments so that less belligerent voices might call for other options, rather than rush into war.

LIFE OVERSHADOWED BY THE GREAT WAR

Like everyone else who lived through the traumas of this time, her life was seriously affected by the war. As the years went by the horror of war and the world-wide unfairness of living conditions affected her deeply. A decade and a half later these thoughts were to surface in her plays, written during the early 1930s.

However, like other women, MDH did what she could to help during the war and she was called upon to undertake some highly-specialised tasks. For some years she had been advising the Town Clerks of Coventry concerning their archives and in 1916 she supervised the removal of the collection to a vault in Lloyds Bank, because of the risk of air-raids. In 1919, after the end of hostilities, she supervised the move back again, so that once again the precious manuscripts were housed in the Muniment Room of St Mary's Hall.

As a sympathetic friend, she was acutely aware of how much suffering the war had caused to many of the families living around her. In 1916 in the Battle of the Somme there was a great loss of life amongst men of the Warwickshire Regiment and there were many houses in her area of Leamington in which the occupants were in deep mourning for husbands, fathers and sons. She was deeply moved by this.

After the war had ended and she wrote many articles about Warwickshire villages for newspapers, she always made a point of remarking on how many names were listed on the Village War Memorial, as if the least a historian could do was give those who lost their lives an honourable mention.

WOMEN'S SUFFRAGE ON HOLD

The cause of women's suffrage was placed on hold during the First World War for as increasing numbers of men went to fight in France and elsewhere, women took over many of the essential jobs. What was unthinkable before the war was soon regarded as inevitable once it was over, for it was perceived that the role of women had changed dramatically.

However that did not mean that men were suddenly converted to the cause of women's emancipation and for MDH and others there were many battles ahead on that front.

THE COVENTRY CITY GUILD

In the spring of 1914, although war was imminent, few realised its proximity and life in England went on very much as before. In Coventry MDH and others carried out a plan in response to suggestions that various of the town's mediaeval buildings should be demolished to make way for wider roads and modern properties.

A notice was issued concerning the setting up of a City Guild. The notice read,

"It has been thought desirous to form a Society on the lines of the Stratford - upon-Avon Guild to preserve those Antiquities of Coventry which are not under the care of the Corporation and to influence, where possible, the artistic development of the city."

The meeting, which was chaired by Colonel Wyley, took place on Tuesday May 26th 1914 at 3.p.m. in the Mayoress's Parlour in St Mary's Hall. The two speakers were Frederick Wellstood of Stratford-upon-Avon and Mary Dormer Harris.

Over thirty people attended the meeting and a report in the "Coventry Standard" a few days later carried many details of the speeches. After Mr Wellstood had described the Stratford-upon-Avon Guild, MDH made an inspirational speech which was fully reported in the newspaper.

"Mr Wellstood has spoken to you as a past master in the art of preserving what is beautiful, historic, and dignified, in a town which is the literary capital of the modern world. I come before you with nothing of his experience, with only the enthusiasm of a 'prentice hand, to try and persuade you, to the best of my poor powers, to establish a society to protect what is beautiful, historic and dignified in this busy manufacturing city..."

MDH went on to explain that she felt their aims could best be achieved by acting in a tactful and helpful manner; then she spoke of a historic site close to her heart, which was in great danger.

"The crux of the matter is Palace Yard. The value as a building site must be enormous, but I suppose future generations would pay more for the treasure of its memories......In less flowery language, I should like to see a civic museum in Palace Yard."

Applause interrupted her and after more stirring words, followed by discussions and proposals, a Guild Council was formed. Later a leaflet was prepared stating the aims of the Guild *"For the preservation of historic buildings and places of natural beauty"* and setting out the objects and rules. On this first leaflet Malcolm Pridmore Esq, JP, Mayor of Coventry, was the President and amongst the nine Vice-Presidents, alongside such names as Lord Leigh and the Lord Bishop of Worcester was that of Mary Dormer Harris, the only woman.

WORKING WITH THE WRITER ANGELA BRAZIL

On that same Coventry City Guild leaflet, the name of the Honorary Secretary was Miss Brazil of 1 The Quadrant, Coventry. Angela Brazil, the famous writer of stories for girls, had come to Coventry in 1911 with her brother, medical practitioner Dr Walter Brazil, and both wanted to take an active role in the new City Guild.

In the early years, some of the numerous committee meetings were held in their house in the Quadrant. Dr Walter ran his medical practice from there and as his chief hobby was repairing old clocks, the house was soon crammed full with interesting specimens, most of which chimed frequently.

ANGELA BRAZIL, THE FAMOUS WRITER OF STORIES FOR GIRLS, WAS THE FIRST SECRETARY OF THE COVENTRY CITY GUILD IN 1914. There was talk of rivalry between her and Mary Dormer Harris and certainly the two women seemed to be vastly different in character.

Both Dr Walter and Angela Brazil were also enthusiastic members of the Natural History and Scientific Society and both were on the committee of that Society. Somehow both brother and sister managed to carry on highly-successful professional careers and in 1914, besides undertaking correspondence connected with the City Guild, Angela Brazil had five stories published in annuals for girls, plus two longer books. This was typical of her huge literary output and most years she wrote two or even three, full-length books.

In 1915, Amy Brazil, sister of Angela and Walter, came to Coventry to live with her siblings, and both she and Angela became avid collectors too. Besides being a nurse, Amy was an artist, and numerous paintings, objects collected on holidays and various curios vied for space in the house. Amy Brazil also joined the City Guild, although she did not hold office.

RIVALRY WITH ANGELA BRAZIL?

It seems rather an unusual occurrence to have two accomplished writers, from two vastly-differing genres, working alongside one another on the same sub-committee. Both were a similar age, Mary Dormer Harris being two years older than Angela Brazil, and with the one being so well established as a serious scholar and historian in the city and the other a newcomer who liked to be the centre of attention, there must have been some friction, even if it generally remained hidden below the surface.

In her biography of Angela Brazil "The Schoolgirl Ethic", published in 1976, Gillian Freeman suggested that there was rivalry between the two writers and it may have aroused jealousy in Angela Brazil that MDH was cast in a leading role whatever she did in Coventry because of her great eloquence, enthusiasm and previous books about the city.

In appearance and character the two women were vastly different. Angela Brazil was tall and preferred to wear soft loose dresses of pale mauve, with shoes and hats with bows or other trims, whereas on the other hand MDH was shorter, wore glasses and did not seem to attach that much importance to dress. She usually wore plain clothes, often of a dark colour, especially as she grew older.

COLLABORATION ON A BOOK LISTING INTERESTING OLD BUILDINGS

Amongst the Coventry City Guild collection in Coventry City Archive Office, is an interesting manuscript book of rough notes, compiled largely by MDH, with contributions by Angela Brazil, Mrs Mitchell Smith and occasionally others. Mostly completed in 1915 it lists and describes in some detail the various ancient buildings in Coventry, and it provided the basis for a more formal Conservation List decades later.

The members of the new society must have realised that publicity and the winning over of public opinion was to play a large part in the success of their venture, and in March 1915 MDH wrote an article for "Country Life" describing the activities of the Guild.

ON NOVEMBER 21st 1921 (according to the date on this photograph) THE MUSEUM ORGANIZED BY THE COVENTRY CITY GUILD MOVED TO BETTER PREMISES IN THE FORMER BABLAKE SCHOOL. This photograph marks that opening and shows the Mayor of Coventry (centre, holding hat) with Lord Leigh next to him and Angela Brazil, with a handbag and fur-stole, centre-right. The tall man next to Angela may well be Dr Walter Brazil and further towards the right of the group, it would appear that the slightly shorter figure in a plain tweed suit, with her hands by her sides, is Mary Dormer Harris.

COVENTRY CITY GUILD HAVE A MUSEUM

The Museum which MDH referred to in her inaugural speech in 1914 never did materialise in Palace Yard in Coventry, although the picturesque buildings were afterwards refurbished and used for meetings. Whether there was rivalry or not between Angela Brazil and MDH, the Coventry City Guild proved an effective society and did a great amount of good in making the public aware of the great architectural heritage which Coventry possessed. At first the Guild had a room in St Mary's Hall for use as Museum and they received many gifts of artefacts to put on show. Later in 1921 the Museum moved to the old Bablake School and these premises served them well for some years.

LEAMINGTON LITERARY SOCIETY

The Leamington Literary and Philosophical Society was founded in 1912 and for the first three and half years proceedings were for men only and of a serious nature. However at the 4th Annual General Meeting on 8th May 1916 two important changes were made. The word "Philosophical" was dropped from the name of the society and it was decided to open the society to any who wished to join, which meant that women were now allowed to become members. Some of the founder members had resisted allowing women to join, but when membership began to fall during the war, it was realized that the change was inevitable.

On October 2nd 1916, another meeting resolved that three people should be approached to give papers to the society and one of these three was MDH. Thus she became the first woman to address the Leamington Literary Society as it had then become and her subject was "Warwickshire Life in Shakespeare's Day."

The local press gave a short report on the proceedings, rather shorter one suspects than if the speaker had been male. One local paper said, *"The lecture dealt with the conditions of country life and education in Shakespeare's day and the error of supposing that such conditions were unfavourable to a poet's growth. Miss Dormer Harris showed that Shakespeare was born at the right time; when the old religious culture of the church met the new culture derived from the newly rediscovered classics. She gave evidence of the contemporary interest in music and acting and of the stores of material to be gathered from folk tales and folk plays. There was no reason to suppose that boys in Shakespeare's class and circumstances had not the opportunity of receiving a good education."*

At this same meeting several women were voted in as members and a few months later, on Monday April 2nd 1917 MDH and a Miss Bevan were both elected members of the society.

"NO EQUAL AS A LECTURER ON BYGONE WARWICKSHIRE"

A few weeks after this at the 5th AGM on April 30th 1917 MDH was elected a member of the committee, and on 10th December 1917 she gave another talk to the Leamington Literary Society on "Historical Local Documents" making special reference to parish registers, wills and title deeds.

As was usually the case, the lecture was reported in the local press, but this time one paper gave as glowing a report as one could wish to find.

"Miss Dormer Harris we should say, has no equal as a lecturer on bygone Warwickshire. A few others may rival her for profundity of research, but she alone posseses the knack of vitalising the dry-as-dust by sparks of humour and by illustrations gathered from the wealth of her experience."

At that period the meetings of the society were held at the Café Royal in Bath Street and MDH spoke to a packed audience.

A year later on 16th December 1918 Mr H. Crouch Batchelor (President of the Baconian Society) spoke to the Literary Society in Leamington, putting the case for Sir Francis Bacon's authorship of Shakespeare's plays. As one might expect in the discussion which followed MDH had plenty to say. She remarked that there was a great deal of evidence from his contemporaries that Shakespeare wrote the plays, and at the end of the evening no one in the room agreed with the speaker.

From time to time MDH gave other talks to the Leamington Literary Society and she gained the position of being very much an elder statesman amongst the members.

FORMATION OF WOMEN'S INSTITUTES

In 1915 Women's Institutes were begun and soon there were branches set up in many towns and villages. MDH heartily approved of this because she felt that as all women were eligible for membership, then all women, married or unmarried, could benefit. In one newspaper article about Ashow some years later she wrote,

"Perhaps it is because the place is so small that there is no village institute there. (Miss Golden, of the Warwickshire Federation of Women's Institutes please note!) There is a Men's Club... and a Mothers' Union, but to the latter spinsters are not eligible for membership. I am all out for making life agreeable for spinsters."

THE WAR ENDS AND WOMEN ARE GIVEN THE VOTE

After the end of the Great War on November 11th 1918, Lloyd George, the Prime Minister, fulfilled his pledge of calling an immediate General Election. This took place on December 28th 1918 and for the first time women over 30 were allowed to vote. It is to be hoped that MDH's mother, then aged 84, was well enough to visit the polling-station for she too had supported the Suffragist cause.

AS A COMMITTED PACIFIST, MARY DORMER HARRIS MUST HAVE REJOICED WHEN THE PEACE TO END THE FIRST WORLD WAR WAS DECLARED IN NOVEMBER 1918. This photograph shows the crowd outside Leamington Town Hall on that happy occasion.

I dare say however that MDH, as she cast her vote, was well aware that the Votes for Women campaign was anything but over. In fact it was to take almost another ten years for all women over 21 to be given the vote when the Franchise Bill was passed on March 29th 1928.

THE ROYAL HISTORICAL SOCIETY IN 1920 AND A NEW BOOK IN 1921

On April 8th 1920 MDH read a paper to the Royal Historical Society entitled "Unpublished Documents relating to Town Life in Coventry". This was later published in the transactions of the society and it also appeared as a separate pamphlet.

In 1921 MDH wrote to Cecil Sharp, the authority on and collector of folk songs, to ask permission to include his "Jack Hale" in her forthcoming book. He sent a handwritten note back from 4 Maresfield Gardens, Hampstead London N.W.3. on 19th February 1921 saying that he had not the slightest objection.

"A SOCIAL AND INDUSTRIAL HISTORY OF ENGLAND"

Of all the books which MDH wrote this seems to be by far the rarest and most obscure. Extensive searches on the Internet by a bookseller friend have failed to locate anything and the nearest I have come to a copy are photocopies of a couple of introductory pages, kindly supplied by a friend with connections to the Bodleian Library in Oxford.

It would appear that the book was one of a series in "A Social and Industrial History of England" and that MDH wrote the volume subtitled "Before the Industrial Revolution." Published by Collins' Clear Type Press, the small illustrated book had 227 pages and was aimed at undergradutes and older students who were already earning their own living.

With its emphasis on economic matters, the book appears to have gone the way of other superseded text-books and now few copies can be found outside the copyright deposit libraries.

A "Special Introduction" by Sir William Ashley (Vice-Principal of the University of Birmingham) paid a great compliment to MDH.

"The present volume is written by one of the very few English scholars who have made protracted and intensive study of mediaeval society, especially of the development of our towns. But Miss Dormer Harris carries her antiquarian learning lightly, she has a keen eye to the things that really mattered. Her readers will be carried along by the contagion of her own vivid interest in the daily life of our forefathers, and they will understand the present all the better for having something to compare it with."

The first sentence of the opening chapter of the book is, in my opinion, as good a definition of history as will be found anywhere.

"History is an account of the doings of men and women of yesterday and all the yesterdays beyond that which make up the past."

Having had my appetite whetted, I look forward to being able to read the whole book some day.

FORMATION OF THE WARWICK AND LEAMINGTON DRAMATIC STUDY CLUB

On 5th May 1922 a group of eighteen people gathered in a house called "Inisfree" in Woodcote Road, Warwick with the idea of founding a Dramatic Study Club. The house belonged to the Rev. and Mrs W.A. Constable and on that first evening a committee of ten people was elected. From the beginning MDH was one of the members of that committee and a few months later she became Vice President. She remained a committee member for the rest of her life; for much of the time being Vice President also.

The object of the club was defined as being *"the study of the Drama and the reading and performance of plays."* The club met alternate Monday evenings and membership cost 2/6 per annum. The first few meetings were in private houses, but later the venue was the Clarendon Hall in Clarendon Street, Leamington Spa and the name of the group was changed to the "Leamington and Warwick Dramatic Study Club."

MRS BARTHWICK IN "THE SILVER BOX"

On Saturday 24th March 1923 at 7.30 p.m. a performance of "The Silver Box" by John Galsworthy took place in Spencer Street Congregational School Hall, Leamington, and MDH played the part of Mrs Barthwick. With a cast of 16 it meant that many of the original members had a part, but in MDH's case it must have been a little difficult for her elderly mother, then 89 years old, was becoming very frail. In all probability MDH had to find a family member or friend to sit with her mother while she was out in the evenings.

DEATH OF MRS HARRIS

On May 15th 1923 MDH's mother died at the age of 89. The obituary in the "Leamington Spa Courier" gave a sympathetic picture of Mrs Harris.

"By her lively interest she did much to stimulate and make possible the historical researches of Miss Dormer Harris. A woman of simple tastes, she was very active in her daily life... Independent thought characterized her in a marked degree; we may recall the occasion when she stood on the kerb in the street and waved to the procession of women suffragists who made a pilgrimage through Leamington in the pre-war days."

Tribute was paid to the wonderful memory of Mrs Harris and it was said that she could remember watching the celebrations in Leamington for the Coronation of Queen Victoria from a balcony overlooking Bath Street, from what was then Woodhouse's shop. Other events which she could vividly recall were the Great Exhibition of 1851 and the visit of Queen Victoria and Prince Albert to Stoneleigh Abbey and Aston Hall in June 1858. From her mother, MDH would have had first-hand accounts of a good many occurrences in Warwickshire and this must have been a help to her when writing about the past.

The obituary of her mother ended with the sentence,

"She had a quiet beloved old age and she will be very much missed."

LIVING ON INVESTMENTS

Mary Harris's will was a relatively simple one and the only beneficiary was her daughter, who was sole executor. It would appear that both MDH and her mother had some small investments and that they lived mainly on the income. Some years later it was said of MDH,

"A political creed was for her no mere subject for discussion; if investments did not satisfy her standard, she and her mother sold out, no matter what the loss."

Few at that or any other time, were sufficiently idealistic to make what are today called "ethical investments". However there is no doubt that both women had an active social conscience which dictated many of their unselfish acts.

HER DARLING MOTHER

Most of MDH's books had been dedicated to her mother, but perhaps her love was best described in her simple verse "IF". This was probably intended as a parody of Kipling's famous poem, but it summarized this period of her life very aptly.

If only winters were never cold,
And darling mothers did not grow old-

If books and tobacco came without cost,
And what one wanted were never lost-

If cups stood always clean on the shelf,
And all the housework performed itself-

If friends dwelt within a minute's walk
Forever ready to listen and talk-

If back and head were never tired,
And one wrote verses as if inspired-

If life were so delicious as that
I should have nothing to grumble at.

In the summer of 1923, MDH had the unwelcome task of going through her mother's possessions, and from time to time sad reminders of the past resurfaced. One such instance she later described in the essay "Travelling Light". Surely she wrote this piece at the time when she was sorting through her mother's drawers and found items which had belonged to her little brother who had died almost fifty years previously?

"The dead child's roughly-cut whistle, the story book he loved, these are the things the mother hardly dares to finger. They lie apart in the drawer until she, too, has taken the last look."

Whatever else she was, respected scholar, gifted lecturer and admired writer, there was no doubt that MDH had been particularly close to her mother, in thought, word and deed, and that she felt her loss very deeply.

6. A GOLDEN PERIOD 1924 -1935

"UNKNOWN WARWICKSHIRE" PUBLISHED 1924

Although she was very far from being wealthy and often needed to supplement her income by writing newspaper articles, from 1924 onwards Mary Dormer Harris seemed to enter a productive and enjoyable period in her life. Her most popular book was published, she gave some prestigious lectures and it was easier for her to travel to visit old friends in Oxford, Cambridge or London.

"Unknown Warwickshire", published by John Lane, The Bodley Head, and illustrated by the Leamington artist and photographer J.E. Duggins, was by the far the most attractive and best known of MDH's works. The lively text was accompanied by plenty of black and white line drawings, as well as twenty colour plates of original paintings. This made the larger size, royal-blue, hardback book, a joy to read and own and even today it is a sought-after book.

IN "UNKNOWN WARWICKSHIRE" PUBLISHED IN 1924, MARY DORMER HARRIS CALLED LEAMINGTON ".. A GENTLE BACKWATER OF A PLACE.." AND SHE MAY HAVE HAD SCENES LIKE THIS IN MIND WHEN SHE WROTE THOSE WORDS. Here Linden Avenue is pictured in Edwardian times in the first decade of the twentieth century, but it changed relatively little in the years which followed.

MARY DORMER HARRIS WROTE OF WHITNASH "...OF THE ANCIENT ELM BEFORE THE THE CHURCH, ONLY THE STUMP IS LEFT..."
This photograph, taken in the later 1920s or early 1930s, shows the old elm, still growing vigorously, behind the war-memorial.

Although she was a long-standing resident of the town, it did not mean that MDH was entirely complimentary about Leamington Spa. I wonder how long it was before her neighbours, living like her, close to St Mark's Church, forgave her for the following somewhat "tongue in cheek" remarks on page 147.

"The best centre for sightseeing in Warwickshire is undoubtedly Leamington, a gentle back-water of a place, where people with not very much to do, and not very much to spend, pass a cosy, church-going existence."

After grumbling that many old street names had been lost in Cubbington, MDH gave out a general plea.

"Why can't people let old things, names and places, bide?"

WHITNASH

I have a specially soft spot for the passage about Whitnash for I quoted this in my first book on that town and I chose a title "Beneath the Great Elms" which reflected MDH's words.

"When I last walked to Whitnash, the great elms were still splendid with leaves but roaring and rocking in the autumn storm... Of the ancient elm before the church, only the stump of the trunk is left. Whitnash has great black and white barns with bulging sides, and the thatch coated with velvet moss and the lichen-covered tiles showed a thousand hues in the sunlight."

KENILWORTH

What Mary Dormer Harris did to Leamington, she also did to Kenilworth, a town she knew well from her youth.

"Everyone goes to Kenilworth, which in my younger days was, like Cranford, in the hands of Amazons, widows and spinsters but is now a flourishing little town and a haunt of business men. As I remember it, district visiting occupied the working hours of the ladies, while relaxation was afforded by prolonged discussions, which only heart-stirring events, like a royal marriage, could divert from local topics, such as the curate's ill-advised attentions to some young lady, whose connections were engaged in retail trade; but we live now under George V and in a changed world."

STRATFORD CHURCH

Some descriptions in "Unknown Warwickshire" are of very well-known places, but MDH manages to make us look at them afresh. Her description of Stratford Church is quite timeless and beautiful.

"It is the church, tower and spire, and the river and trees that make Stratford so beautiful, and we must be thankful that a public spirit beyond praise has kept fields and gardens nearby free from the encroachments of the builder. It is good to

IN "UNKNOWN WARWICKSHIRE" MARY DORMER HARRIS HAD PLENTY OF PRAISE FOR STRATFORD-UPON-AVON.

sit on the low stone churchyard wall, looking out on the river and its reflections, or turning back to see how the fine chancel rises above the crowd of undistinguishable graves."

HONORIFICABILITUDINITATIBUS

An interesting curiosity from Pillerton Hersey crops up in one of Shakespeare's plays and MDH describes it in some detail in Chapter Two.

"The registers of Pillerton, which date from 1539, enshrine by a scribe's casual scribble, the monster word honorificabilitudinitatibus, thereby attaining to some small celebrity among those learned in trifles of Shakespearean lore. The word occurs in "Love's Labours Lost" V.i,...Costard, the country clown, says to Moth, Armado's small, precocious page,

'I marvel thy master hath not eaten thee for a word; for thou art not so long by the head as honorificabilitudinitatibus: thou art easier swallowed than a flap-dragon.

There are people who imagine the use of this absurdity to be an effort of scholarship beyond the reach of an unlettered country clown such as the Stratford poet. One of them thinking that the word contained a hitherto undiscovered cryptic message concerning the Baconian authorship evolved from its polysyllabic store the anagram: 'Hi ludi F. Baconis nati tuiti orbi: These plays, F. Bacon's offspring, are preserved to the world.' The fact that the Pillerton scribe chose this long-tailedness to try his pen upon shows the word was generally (and locally) known in Shakespeare's day."

BURTON DASSETT

MDH could also describe atmosphere very well as she did when writing of Burton Dassett.

"It is a lonesome place. Burton Dassett is the strangest village of any in the shire. Village did I say? There was a village once, I suppose, but now there stand on the hill with fair prospect, nothing but a dark grey church, a vicarage, a holy well, a windmill, a forsaken quarry and a fifteenth century beacon house. In old time I am sure there was a gallows. People talk of ghosts here, but rationalists will have the curious lights, sometimes visible, to be nothing but marsh fires, the will o' the wisp."

PARISH CLERKS

MDH had much time for Parish Clerks and she paid them the handsomest of compliments at the end of Chapter Twenty-eight.

Of parish clerks in general she said *"His talk, when he lets himself go, is usually sound as a nut in October, for while it is not uncommon for a man to finish his course at either of the major universities and remain a fool at last, it is rare to find a parish clerk who is not - in the eighteenth century phrase - a man of parts...."*

GEORGE ELIOT

MDH was always very interested in George Eliot and she tried to assess the novelist's reputation.

"Do people read "Adam Bede" now? Trollope has come into his own. Dickens with his marvellous creative vitality seems to be acknowledged chief of the Victorians, but the memory of George Eliot has grown somewhat dim in these later years... It may be that her melancholy prevents her from making way with a generation that loves mirth and a light touch. Certainly she is the saddest of authors....Perhaps only poets, for poetry purges the soul with pity, should touch on a theme that breaks the heart."

BIRMINGHAM LIBRARY

MDH obviously had happy memories of the library in Birmingham.

"There are pleasant places in New Birmingham, the Reference Library, for instance, where books are delivered quite quickly, a Paradise for those with a point to look up, just in the half- hour before the departure of the country train."

As I too have always found the librarians in the Central Library to be extremely helpful, I was delighted to read that comment.

WARWICK

The section on Warwick begins with a classic, fact-packed sentence.

"Warwick stands on its rock, quiet and feudal, with two church-crowned gates, one at each end of a little street, a timbered hospital, once the hall of the guild of the Holy Trinity and St George, classic houses at street corners built after the fire of 1694, and far, far too much history behind it to be compressed into a little space."

A typically informative, yet amusing section concerned St Mary's Church.

"In the chancel lies Thomas Beauchamp, who fought at Poitiers, and in the Beauchamp Chapel lies his grandson, Richard, governor of Henry VI, adversary of the Maid of Orleans, under a tomb of rare splendour, made of "latten," or gilt bronze, and Purbeck marble. Latten was at one time a metal in common use, hence the point of Shakespeare's - probable apocryphal - jest, when he stood sponsor to a child of the learned Ben Jonson. 'I will give my godson a Latin spoon,' he said, 'and thou, Ben, shalt translate it.'
...The Beauchamp Chapel...is one of the most complete and wonderful of the mediaeval chantry chapels left in England. All the thought and devotion and art of the time are brought into this small space."

LOVE OF COVENTRY

However enthusiastic MDH was about other places, it was obvious that it was Coventry which held the key to her heart. In Chapter Twenty-two she wrote two sentences which sum up the Coventry of the twenty first century as well as the city of eighty years previously.

THE TOMB OF RICHARD BEAUCHAMP IN THE BEAUCHAMP CHAPEL IN ST MARY'S CHURCH IN WARWICK. An illustration similar to this appeared in "Unknown Warwickshire."

"The more I write of Coventry the less I am able to put into words the spell it casts on those who love it.

In this wonderful place the old and new are inextricably mixed together..."

She goes on to explain,

"Beautiful houses are to be seen everywhere, in Butcher Row, a mediaeval thoroughfare, apparently doomed, though it has still escaped the improver's rage, in Cross Cheaping and Broadgate....

...Perhaps the greatest treasure is Ford's Hospital, founded in 1529, where a door through a gabled and timbered frontage leads into an oblong courtyard."

Sometimes MDH gives her readers something to ponder. Of Trinity Church, Coventry she wrote,

"The architecture of Trinity with its fourteenth century nave arcade is very impressive and it is hard to say whether this, or Warwick, is the most beautiful town church of the shire."

"BEAUTIFUL HOUSES ARE TO BE SEEN EVERYWHERE, IN BUTCHER ROW, A MEDIAEVAL THOROUGHFARE, APPARENTLY DOOMED, THOUGH IT HAS STILL ESCAPED THE IMPROVER'S RAGE, IN CROSS CHEAPING AND BROADGATE..."

So wrote Mary Dormer Harris of Coventry in 1924. This drawing, by Florence Weston, completed in the 1920s, shows Trinity Lane, with the rear of houses in Butcher Row to the left. The familiar half-timbered building facing is in Priory Row, and Trinity Churchyard is behind the railings to the right

THIS VIEW OF COVENTRY, LOOKING DOWN BROADGATE TOWARDS CROSS CHEAPING, IN THE LATE 1920s, MUST HAVE BEEN VERY FAMILIAR TO MARY DORMER HARRIS. Although she occasionally rode in them, she disliked motor-cars and indeed all things mechanical.

THE DUGDALE SOCIETY

The Dugdale Society had been formed in 1920 for the preservation and publication of manuscripts which would add to the history of Warwickshire, and on Saturday 25th October 1924 MDH read a paper to the Dugdale Society at St Mary's Hall, Coventry. Her title was "The Ancient Records of Coventry" and in the audience were an impressive array of scholars, historians and local dignitaries.

The Mayor of Coventry presided and Mr F.C. Wellstood, FSA, Director of the Shakespeare Birthplace Trust and Secretary of the Dugdale Society, assisted. Also present were three other Fellows of the Society of Antiquaries including her friend Philip Chatwin; two headmasters of important local secondary schools; an Inspector of Schools; three Chief Librarians of towns or cities; Edward Hicks, the Editor of the "Leamington Spa Courier"; and the writer Angela Brazil plus other members of the Coventry City Guild.

It took an excellent speaker to satisfy an audience like that and proof of MDH's skill came from the differences in the text of the speech when published by the Dugdale Society as "Occasional Paper Number One," and the speech as reported in the Coventry Standard of 1st November 1924. The following passage is missing from the published paper, perhaps because it poked fun at members of the Dugdale Society, including MDH herself. When describing how some documents were scattered over the city in lawyer's offices, she said they were *"guarded by people who had something better to do in a solid business way than minister to the wants of eccentric persons who wish to read ancient writings."*

I feel sure that at that moment, her speech was interrupted by laughter.

THE HISTORY OF THE DRAPERS COMPANY OF COVENTRY

In 1926 a small book was published which dealt entirely with the history of the influential Drapers Company in Coventry. Details of the mystery plays performed in the streets of the city until 1580 were given and, as MDH said, Shakespeare may well have witnessed performances.

"For some two hundred years the people of Coventry and the country round kept holiday on the feast of Corpus Christi, the day before the Great Fair, and went out to see the religious or 'mystery' plays performed in the streets of the city. These plays, supported by the contributions of the various crafts, were performed on two-roomed, wheeled stages, drawn by hired men from one convenient spot to another, each show being repeated, it seems, three times. ... Indeed the poet may well have seen it for does he not say in his ribald manner how the sight of a flea at the end of Bardolf's inflamed nose struck Falstaff with its likeness to a black soul in the fires of hell? (Hen. V. Act. ii. Sc. iii).

...The 'damned' souls with blackened faces and flame-like hose of yellow and red, would be seen going down towards the great dragon-like jaws of hell whence issued flames of fire..."

LECTURER AT THE UNIVERSITY OF BIRMINGHAM

From 1927 to 1931 MDH was Local History Lecturer at the University of Birmingham. It was a part-time post, possibly involving one day a week, and in her first year she delivered a series of lectures on "Local Mediaeval and Sixteenth Century History." In subsequent years she gave lectures on mediaeval trade and industry, the growth of guilds and craft mystery plays. Many of the lectures were illustrated with lantern-slides and she also arranged archaeological excursions.

Her lectures were a resounding success, no doubt because she was such an interesting personality and had spent many years devoted to research of her subject. A number of her students were so impressed with her lectures that they afterwards became firm friends.

The Archivist (Special Collections) at the University of Birmingham has been good enough to send me details of the History School for the period 1927-1932 and without exception, all other lecturers, apart from MDH, list their degrees. I could not understand why MDH had not been granted a retrospective degree in 1920 when women were officially admitted to degrees, until I discovered from a friend that the Final Honours School in English Language and Literature before 1895 was not recognised. To me it seemed ironic that such a learned and scholarly person as MDH should have been refused a retrospective degree.

WHEN ALMOST SIXTY YEARS OLD, MARY DORMER HARRIS BECAME LOCAL HISTORY LECTURER AT THE UNIVERSITY OF BIRMINGHAM AND THIS PHOTOGRAPH SHOWS THE HISTORY STUDENTS FELLOWSHIP IN 1927. Miss Dormer Harris is second from right on the front row, whilst in the centre is Sir Raymond Beazley (Professor of History from 1909 - 1933) and Lady Beazley. Lecturer Dorothy Sutcliffe, who later married Philip Styles, is next to Lady Beazley.

IN HER LECTURES MDH OFTEN DESCRIBED MISERICORDS. This recent photograph shows one of these mediaeval hinged-seats in the choir of Holy Trinity Church, Coventry. The carving depicts a closed door, emblematic of the virginity of the Virgin Mary, with supporters of roses on either side.

HISTORY FELLOWSHIP IN LATER YEARS

Even after she had left her position at The University of Birmingham in 1932, MDH sometimes joined in the social activities of the History Students' Fellowship. One young friend, R.G. Slater, recalled that in November 1933 MDH and Philip Styles (who had taken over the post of Lecturer in Local History in 1932 on her recommendation) went to a dance at the History School. Philip *"capered about nicely with all the young ladies"* while MDH, then aged sixty-six, sat sedately by *"as befits my age and figure"* as she explained. Ronald Slater continued about 'Dor' as they called her.

"But it was not to be. Up comes the President and says 'If we have a Polka will you dance?' Dor agrees, and throwing age and figure to the winds, does so. Also Sir Roger de Coverley, like Queen Elizabeth showing off before the ambassador. Coming back they almost missed the train, and would have done had not Miss Dormer Harris appeared at the gentlemen's dressing room in a pair of galoshes and in a rude hurry extracted her friend."

BIRMINGHAM ARCHAEOLOGICAL SOCIETY

As long ago as 1899 MDH had read a paper to the Birmingham Archaeological Society and especially during the 1920s and 1930s this contact continued. Her friend Philip Chatwin, diocesan architect, and noted archaeologist, often wrote papers of his own for the academic journals and sometimes during the 1920s MDH would accompany him to various sites of interest. Occasionally, these excursions were organised by the Birmingham Archaeological society. There was a growing interest in history and archaeology in the 1920s and in those grim, post-war days many more people took up hiking and more became aware of local historical sites.

THE COVENTRY CITY GUILD CONTINUES

Throughout the 1920s the Coventry City Guild continued to flourish with MDH and Angela Brazil as prime movers in the organisation, alongside other prominent citizens.

If there was rivalry between the two writers, it was not apparent in a note in the Coventry City Guild Collection, now in Coventry City Archives. Dated March 30th 1924, the note from MDH read,

"Dear Miss Brazil,

Here is the book with some odd notes I thought I had better not destroy.

I hope you have recovered from your illness.

With kind regards,

Yours sincerely,

M. Dormer Harris"

It rather sounded as if the book was the manuscript book they had compiled in 1915, but it might have been many other things.

In 1931 Angela Brazil tendered her resignation as Secretary and it was MDH who made the speech of thanks. She said that they were all very glad that Miss Brazil was not severing her connection with the Guild and she did not think they would have had a museum if it had not been for her.

Also at the Annual Meeting of the Guild in 1931, MDH gave a talk, illustrated with lantern slides on the subject of "Coventry Treasures and their Preservation." The meeting was held in the St James Room of the then-refurbished Palace Yard, and in her talk MDH expressed the hope that Priory Row would never fall into the hands of a speculator for it was in the nature of being a Cathedral Close.

THE IVORY CAR AND OTHER STORIES AND ARTICLES

During the 1920s and 1930s MDH wrote an increasing number of articles for the "Coventry Herald", with occasional contributions to the "Leamington Spa Courier" and other local papers, national magazines and periodicals. Whilst many articles had a historical basis, MDH sometimes wrote more imaginative pieces such as "The Ivory Car" first published on December 23rd & 24th 1927 in the "Coventry Herald".

MDH's great social conscience and Christian compassion underlies the content of "The Ivory Car." No one is forgotten in this Christmas fantasy; old women sitting by the fire *(give them a "pre-war crimson shawl...and see if the coal-box needs replenishing")*, nurses and mothers who have been wakened so often they forget to sleep, people who think they are sinful and those that lie in pain.

Perhaps the most emotive paragraph is when the lonely are comforted and you wonder whether, despite having numerous friends, MDH felt lonely after the death of her mother, for she lived alone and her closest relations were cousins.

"There happens the most unbelievable thing in all the world. For in a flash the room, which was but half full, is crowded by a great company, to you invisible. But others do see for they stand transfigured, with eyes love-lit...and you realize that they are all momentarily gazing on beloved faces they never hoped to see again."

"SHALL I SEE YOU HOME?"

Concerning the delivery of the newspaper articles written during this period, a delightful anecdote was recalled by the late Gertrude Bark. MDH often worked late into the night if her deadline for delivery to the "Coventry Herald" loomed and on one occasion she was especially late. She finished writing the article around three o'clock in the morning, then dashed round to put the precious manuscipt through the letter-box of her friend Herbert Jenkins, who lived nearby in the Rugby Road. He worked in the Midland Bank in Coventry and the plan was that he would deliver the article before beginning work that morning.

However, as MDH turned from the letter-box, she found herself face to face with a policeman, on his nightly beat.

"Good morning! Not a usual time to be out, madam, is it? Shall I see you home?"

Gertrude Bark did not finish the story, except to remark that MDH made her way home, presumably alone, her *"tired eyes twinkling behind her spectacles, hands deep in the pockets of her battered dark-grey coat."*

UNPUBLISHED ESSAYS

In the 1930s MDH also wrote several other essays which as far as I am aware, remained unpublished until after her death. One of these was entitled "Travelling Light" and the last paragraph described Charlie the white horse she remembered so fondly from her childhood.

"...He came from the wide, wolf-haunted plains of Russia, and for many years drew the old pony carriage... He would trot on mildly and patiently, without a quiver, for miles along the rose-scented lanes to Stratford. It was a longish drive, and to give him a rest we always baited at Sherbourne... Shakespeare's town is always there, and if you go at a quiet time it keeps something of the old enchantment, but the Past cannot give back the slow drive through the lanes in all their sweetness and the sound of the plop-plop of Charlie's hoofs along the pleasant road."

Another essay concerned "Meals" and MDH acknowledged her love for good puddings.

"It is a cardinal maxim that one should be early on days when there is treacle pudding to be had, this vanishes so fast, and I have often wondered why at restaurants one cannot have roly-poly made exclusively with black-currant jam, mere plum is a preserve of such relative insignificance."

MDH OFTEN MENTIONED CHARLIE, THE HORSE SHE REMEMBERED SO WELL FROM HER CHILDHOOD.

COMPASSION FOR OTHERS

In the more affluent atmosphere of today, we are apt to forget how short money was for many in the late 1920s and 1930s when unemployment was high and many lacked the necessities of life. In 1931 the pound was devalued and this must have hit people like MDH very hard. Even a small drop in income would have been hard to bear and this may well have been why she found the need to earn more from journalism. However that did not mean that she stopped feeling sorry for others less well-off and her friends noted a succession of regular callers begging small amounts of money.

Family history helps me here for my paternal grandmother, living only half a mile away from MDH, being of a similar age and possessing similar Christian compassion, also helped those who had fallen on hard times by dispensing tea and sympathy as she had little money to give. It would not surprise me to learn that in some instances both she and MDH were helping the same unfortunate people.

A CONTINUED INTEREST IN ACTING

From the late 1920s onward, MDH seemed to have an increased interest in the theatre. When she visited other towns and cities she frequently saw fine performances in the professional theatres. She was friendly with Phyllis Hicks, elder daughter of "Leamington Spa Courier" Editor, Edward Hicks. Phyllis was the drama critic for her father's paper and, despite the forty years difference in their ages and

MDH PLAYED THE PART OF MRS PIERCE IN A PLAY AT THE LOFT THEATRE IN 1933. The photograph of her in costume, was taken in the back garden of her house in Gaveston Road, Leamington.

despite the fact that MDH had sometimes given tuition to Phyllis, the two would attend plays together.

MDH continued to enjoy acting in plays performed by the Leamington and Warwick Dramatic Study Club and in March 1930 she played the part of Ranskaya, in an anti-war play "The Rumour" by C.K. Munroe, performed in the Winter Hall in Leamington. In June 1933 she played Mrs Pierce in a short play "Three and Indivisible" by H.G. Matthews and in 1935 she made three appearances. In May she played Emmie, the servant in Shaw's "The Doctor's Dilemma", in June she was the Good Angel in Marlowe's "Dr Faustus" and in November she played Ftatateeta in "Caesar and Cleopatra," also by Shaw.

In 1932 the Dramatic Study Club had acquired their own premises and the majority of MDH's performances were at this new venue, a former stable at 58A, Bedford Street, Leamington Spa. Since the rented room was a loft, the obvious name for the theatre was "The Loft."

AS SHE HAD A GREAT RESPECT FOR GEORGE BERNARD SHAW, IT MUST HAVE GIVEN MARY DORMER HARRIS GREAT PLEASURE TO PLAY THE PART OF EMMIE IN SHAW'S "THE DOCTOR'S DILEMMA" AT THE LOFT THEATRE IN 1935. Again this photograph was taken in her back garden.

The acquisition of their own theatre had long been a dream of MDH and the rest of the society. At that time membership of the group was around one hundred and the proposal was to perform for an audience of members and friends only, thereby eliminating possible financial losses incurred by the hire of other premises. It was intended that the theatre would be a kind of student theatre where experimental works could be performed, as well as tried and trusted favourites by famous playwrights.

It was a sensible venture which saw membership of the group increase rapidly. By 1936 there were two hundred members and many young and talented people had joined.

"THE WATERS OF FORGETFULNESS" 1933

In 1933 one of MDH's own plays was performed at "The Loft" and as she was such a popular personality, for the week that the play was produced, all records of attendance were broken.

The play appeared to capture the spirit of the 1930s very well. At that time old traditions were dying as more machines took over essential tasks and many people feared the growing threat of war. Philosophical ideas were put forward in the play. and Pudusky, a General in the Bassolonian Army, ominously mentions why many wars are fought.

"In order that a man can peaceably enjoy his own, he must be able to defend it against aggressors. The essence of progress lies in the maintenance of order. In short in the possession - in right hands, of course - of a thick stick."

The Professor (played by Philip Styles) answers,

"I wonder if we can always be sure of chastising the real aggressors, or that what we seek to defend is always absolutely our own."

Those last words from the play will be readily echoed by pacifists the world over, not only in the 1930s but in every age, not least our own, following the events of September 2001.

At the end of the play a Sower of Tares enters, a sinister character who perpetuates evil, and this cameo part was played by Geoffrey Bark, sometime Chairman of the club and husband of Gertrude Bark, who was a great friend of Mary Dormer Harris.

"ST GEORGE AND THE DRAGON" 1934

Another play by MDH "St George and the Dragon" was performed at the Loft Theatre in 1934. With the time and place stated as "anywhere" and the dress stated as "modern" the play is an allegorical, sometimes amusing, piece where the real hero is a blind beggar who dies in the last scene.

During the 1930s a popular actor named Jack Harrison took part in a number of plays at the Loft theatre and later he moved to the Birmingham Rep. In 1934 he played the challenging part of the Dragon; the stage direction describing him as *"an exquisitely got-up young man, in modern dress."*

R.G Slater recalled MDH (whom he knew as Dor) watching a performance of her play at the Loft Theatre.

"There is a certain amount of dissatisfaction with the acting, which served to put Dor in an aggressive mood. 'It is strange that the Lord permits such unmitigated asses to walk the earth... It's so odd. They can't be funny. People do not seem to understand humour. You should hear him say 'my knees positively tremble under me.' It might be 'I don't like rice pudding.'"

However MDH seems to have gone home happy as Mr Bladon Peake of the Crescent Theatre in Birmingham watched the show and said how much he approved of the play, which he was thinking of putting on the following year. She said,

"I feel a little peacocky, but it may come to nothing."

The lines which MDH had felt were badly acted were spoken by the King in the play. Since two actors were alternating with this part, we shall never know whether it was Rev. J.M. Vincent or Eric Andrew who incurred her wrath!

"THE BRIDGE"

When MDH visited Oxford in February 1932 for some medical treatment, one evening there was a gathering of *"the intellectual elite, mostly acting sort of people"* according to a young friend, at MDH's hotel on Boar's Hill, when two of her plays " St George and the Dragon" and "The Bridge" were read aloud. One Oxford friend read awfully well as the dragon, but "The Bridge" went best of all it seems.

However in Cambridge the following year when MDH was visiting an old friend, "The Bridge" was read again. This time it was not appreciated.

"I can't think why you write those mystic things when there are realities to write about" was one comment.

In 1935 a theatrical group from Weston-Super-Mare asked permission to perform "The Bridge". MDH and Leslie Titley of Bristol Road, Weston-Super-Mare had quite a correspondence over the proposed performance and some other groups also expressed interest in her work.

LETTERS FROM SIDNEY AND MARY ADDY

MDH had been friendly for a number of years with Mary and Sidney Addy, whose book "The Evolution of the English House" had been published around 1900 in the same series as her own "Life in an Old English Town". In the Spring of 1933 there was a rapid exchange of letters between Sidney Addy's wife Mary and MDH. Sidney Addy was very ill, their daughter had just died and Mary Addy was vainly trying to sort out financial affairs.

It was evident from the stream of letters from their house in London W2 to *"Our dear Molly"* that MDH was a tower of strength to them in their hour of need. Not only did she offer practical help, but she also tried to give more substantial assistance by doing all she could to help secure a Civil List pension for Sidney. Miss Thomson, a friend of MDH's, had also written letters and visited the family.

To help take their mind off depressing matters, MDH had sent them a copy of her article on Stoneleigh and Mary Addy wrote back,

"I have read a little of your delightful picture of Stoneleigh to him...It is just the kind of writing he loves... He said that more of your writings should eventually be in book form...

I look at your dear mother's portrait from time to time. It is a gentle, intellectual and noble face. Dear - dear Molly! You have to miss her all your life. I realise this more than ever."

Mary Addy obviously knew how hard MDH pushed herself, for the last letter in the series ended with,

"Hoping you are well and not working too hard."

A LETTER TO GERTRUDE BARK IN 1935

Of all her personal letters which I have seen, one which MDH wrote to a great friend, Mrs Gertrude Bark, stands out as being particularly amusing. This letter was written to Mrs Bark, when she was recuperating in the Warneford Hospital, Leamington Spa in July 1935.

In the first paragraph MDH explains how busy she has been working on the guild book. Then the amusing remarks begin to flow.

"We are all well up here, if rather tired. Mrs Styles has been making cakes for a bazaar...I never met a woman who handled things to eat with such skill. I had dinner there on Sunday ...and the gravy! Some people's is like glue. There's nothing like gluey gravy to put you off a meal...

If the Government really knew what was what - which being composed of men it doesn't - it would make Mrs Styles a Minister of Domestic Economy and put her into a house in Downing Street...

...She (referring to Phyllis Hicks) *never wastes time. I am always wasting time, telling myself foolish stories, reading low-brow books, chattering, playing Patience, smoking; losing the diamond-set hours one after another. And it's too late to mend...*

...I love thee just as much as if I wrote to thee every day.

And so farewell"

ALWAYS TREMENDOUSLY BUSY

As her biographer, the remarks about wasting time made by MDH in her letter to Gertrude Bark amused me very much. Even in her late sixties, MDH was full of nervous energy, cramming into each day a huge variety of activities. One hour would be spent playing cribbage, trying to cheer up some cousins who lived nearby, whilst the next would be spent writing about some difficult mediaeval text. She sometimes gave the impression that she was rather scatter-brained because she often lost things like tickets. R.G.Slater described her in 1933.

"She had a lovely time in Malvern; lost gloves and misplaced specs and tickets and had occasional fights and tiffs with the dogmatic young."

However it is clear to me that in reality MDH was entirely focussed and had almost everything under control. Although she encouraged lots of visitors to pop in to her house, if she needed to work she'd make a polite request,

"Now run along there's a dear for I've got another article in the pot."

THOSE ROWDY PARTIES

During the 1930s an ever-increasing band of young students loved to call in on MDH and she gave encouragement and good advice to many. However it was her spontaneous humour which endeared her to them, and the lively play-readings, impromptu games of charades and rowdy parties which often took place were loved by all, except her neighbours.

One of the young visitors, Gertrude Bark, described these parties in her notes.

"How we loved her parties at No 16 Gaveston Road - any excuse would do. After a play reading, out would come the macaroons and bananas and her tiny kitchen would seethe with coffee making. The house would echo with excited and

learned argument by the scholars among us and shrieks of laughter as we plundered it for props for the inevitable games of charades. In one of these the least belligerent of our little group addressed a supposedly left-wing meeting. Her wildly revolutionary speech surprised even us and led to rowdy cheers. Next day we heard MDH's neighbour was petitioning the street to advise the police of the dangerous, traitorous goings-on at Miss Harris's political meetings. 'It ought to be stopped' they said."

From other accounts of this noisy party, it seems it was the lusty singing of "The Red Flag" which led the neighbours in that genteel part of Leamington to think that MDH was a communist sympathiser!

A RADIO PERSONALITY

Her increased interest in the theatre undoubtedly led to MDH's increased interest in dialogue as a means of expressing historical facts and in early 1935 she managed to interest the BBC in her work.

She travelled to London to rehearse some radio talks for the Schools Programmes and a delightful conversation was recalled later by R.G. Slater. He had been present when MDH had had a conversation with Philip Styles about the horrors of performing in an old-fashioned studio.

MDH *Eh I was nervous to a degree. They first of all listened to the two talks, and then they said 'you must talk in your natural voice' (have another gingerbread). As if you could be natural with a horrid thing rather like a dentist's wheel hanging in front of your nose and a green light flashing on and off in the corner to tell you when to speak and when to stop. Philip it was awful...*

Philip *But did they think the talks would do?*

MDH *They want them all dialogue. They were very complimentary about my dialogue, Mr Styles so there...*

Philip *They don't have to listen to so many of your monologues as I do.*

MDH *Philip you rascal. (have another gingerbread or cigarette.) When the rehearsal was over, Mr Dixon the producer (rather a dear) came in and offered me a black currant lozenge. I could only faintly hasp "Have you such a thing as a cigarette about you?*

THE RADIO PROGRAMMES ARE BROADCAST

The first radio programme went out, presumably live, on the National Station on Thursday March 21st 1935 from 11.30 to 11.50 a.m. as part of the Programmes for Schools for the day. The programme was billed as *"Districts of England IX. The Centre of England. A Dramatic Interlude - The Bear and the Ragged Staff"* by Mary Dormer Harris. The playlet illustrated events which took part in Warwick in 1471 and the cast list made interesting reading.

1st Soldier
Town Crier } - *Philip Wade (who also dramatised the work)*

Warwick - Andrew Churchman

The Boy - Brian Bickers

2nd Soldier
Messenger } - *Carlton Hobbs*

The Father - Norman Shelley

The last two names in the list will be familiar to a good many people, for the actors afterwards went on to become famous performers.

The second programme went out a week later on Thursday March 28th 1935. The title this time was *"Shakespeare and Stratford-on-Avon". Districts of England X, The Centre of England -3"*. This time MDH herself was the narrator and she was accompanied by Ivy Parkin. After a dialogue between the narrator and reader, who read short passages from Shakespeare, there followed a shortened version of "A Midsummer Night's Dream" Act 1, scene ii with the four characters Quince, Bottom, Flute and Snug. Since no other actors were mentioned it rather sounded as if MDH and Ivy Parkin read the parts between them.

FEEDBACK FROM SCHOOLCHILDREN

After the transmission of the programmes MDH received some interesting letters from schoolchildren and one particular letter gave her much amusement.

"Dear Madam,

I heard your wireless talk on Shakespeare last week and I want to thank you and say how perfectly lovely it was. How nice it must be for you to have such lovely recollections of Shakespeare."

MDH was delighted and commented,

"The little dears, as if I had walked out with the Immortal one..."

WORKERS' EDUCATIONAL ASSOCIATION

In 1903 a one-time clerk, Albert Mansbridge, set up the Association to Promote the Higher Education of Working Men and he became the first Honorary Secretary. In 1904 the first two branches were set up and in 1905 the association changed its name to the Workers' Educational Association. The idea was to bring together the Co-operative Societies, the trade unions and University Extension and from the onset fair-minded graduates like MDH were fully in support of the scheme which aimed to provide tuition from some of the finest scholars. Many university colleges encouraged the scheme and Government funding later became available.

Gradually branches were set up all over England and a branch opened in Leamington in 1919. MDH did all she could to help and became a Vice President of the Association.

CANVASSING FOR PEACE.

For a number of years MDH had been a staunch supporter of the local League of Nations Association. As a committed pacifist she deeply regretted the terrible slaughter of the Great War.

R.G. Slater recalled that in 1933, when there was a general anti-war mood in Britain, MDH had said,

"Perhaps the war won't break out. I think it unlikely. No one wants it. If half a dozen sensible WOMEN from different countries met and arranged things we could sleep in peace."

In 1935, despite her other heavy commitments she went out canvassing in the cause of peace around election time.

STAUNCH SUPPORTER OF THE LABOUR PARTY

The first time that women were allowed to vote was at the end of 1918 and during the 1920s and 1930s MDH took a great interest in politics. Like many intellectuals of the time, she had been a firm believer in the Labour Party from its earliest days and with other suffragists, she had been grateful for the support given by the Labour Party whenever female emancipation had been discussed.

From a series of letters sent to a young friend Robin Chapman in 1935 we learn a great deal about her sympathies for the Labour Party in the election of that year.

On November 12th 1935 she wrote,

"I have made up what I am pleased to call my mind to vote Labour. Eden pulled hard. I admire the man, but when one has made up one's mind to belong to a party with certain views one should stick to it. Moseley, Simon and McDonald are such melancholy instances of turncoats that they ought to be put in a museum to serve as a warning. Be sure to vote Labour at Cambridge. Philip is urging his friends to vote Labour at Oxford...

...I heard Herbert Morrison and Noel Baker on Sunday at Coventry. Philip took me. The Baths Hall was packed to suffocation and there was an overflow meeting. Meetings however, don't always mean votes. Morrison is very clever, something of an orator, but with the assurance of good work behind him, and has a vein of humour."

In her letter to Robin written on Nov 25th 1935 she reported

"I don't think Labour did badly as far as the votes went. 10,000 in this division was heroic! The weather was bad too. A better distribution of votes would make the parties nearly equal."

THE REGISTER OF THE GUILD OF THE HOLY TRINITY

Although the register had been known to earlier historians, for many years it was thought, wrongly, that the manuscript had been destroyed in the fire at Birmingham Library in 1879. However in 1917 someone alerted MDH to a manuscript which was offered for sale in Bristol and she confirmed that it was

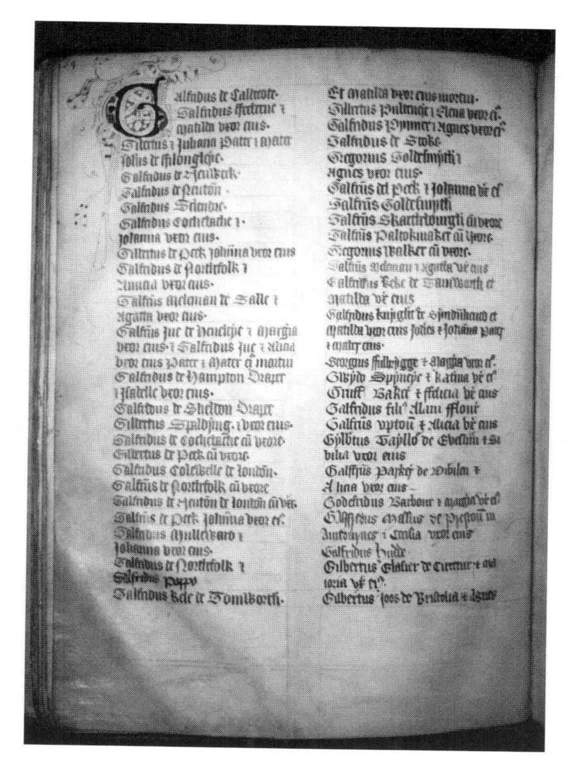

"THE WRITING IS OFTEN DECORATIVE AND INITIAL LETTERS OF IMPORTANT NAMES ARE RUBRICATED."
So wrote Mary Dormer Harris of the Register of the Guild of the Holy Trinity etc. This recent photograph is of one page from that Guild Register, now housed in Coventry City Archives Office.

indeed the missing register of the Coventry Guild. In 1923, after some financial help was given by a Coventry institution, it was purchased by Coventry Corporation on behalf of the city. Then MDH was asked to transcribe it.

However in 1925 MDH had problems. She wrote to the Town Clerk of Coventry *"...my eyes are not at all satisfactory..."* and she suggested that someone else might complete the transcription. Finally she did agree to undertake the work and, as they had with the Leet Book, Coventry Corporation made the necessary arrangements to deposit the book in Leamington Reference Library, for her convenience.

A BEAUTIFUL CODEX

In her 'Introduction' to the transcription MDH gives a detailed description of the volume she had to deal with.

"The codex, bound in ancient leather, which measures 16 in. by 12 in., is made up of 164 folios of parchment, on which are written in fine book-hand of various types belonging to the later fourteenth and first half of the fifteenth century columns of names of those who entered the Guild. The writing is often decorative, and initial letters of important names are rubricated."

AT CHRISTMAS 1933 MDH SENT A COPY OF THIS SNAPSHOT TO PHYLLIS HICKS WITH THE FOLLOWING MESSAGE WRITTEN ON THE BACK.
"Not very good perhaps; but the wall is excellent!"
MDH was a very lively and amusing friend to a number of young people.

As she makes clear, MDH received help from her old friend Mr F.C. Wellstood of Stratford-upon-Avon who was still the Honorary Secretary and General Editor of the Dugdale Society. In thanking Mr Wellstood and his wife, and Miss E. Bamford, for general help, proof-reading and compiling the general index, MDH goes on to concede,

"Without this welcome co-operation I doubt if I could have completed this work."

THANKS TO COVENTRY CORPORATION

In the publication of this book the Mayor and Corporation come out with lavish praise heaped upon them for giving financial assistance. The Special Acknowledgement by the President, Chairman of the Council and the Honorary Secretary and General Editor of the Dugdale Society was given pride of place in the book.

"In issuing this, the thirteenth volume of the publications of the Dugdale Society, acknowledgement must be made to the Mayor and Corporation of Coventry, not only for permission to transcribe and publish the Trinity Guild Register, but also for their generous offer of financial assistance towards the cost of printing it.

On behalf of the Dugdale Society we desire to express our gratitude to them for their munificence which is a testimony of their appreciation of the historical value of the city's records, and of their goodwill in placing them within the reach of students and archaeologists."

"A DULL BOOK OF MINE!"

When the labour of nearly ten years was finally finished, did MDH feel a great sense of pride and achievement? In her heart she must have done so, yet on November 12th 1935 she wrote to Robin Chapman,

"A dull book of mine has come out. History. Manuscripts. Coventry. About 2 people seem to like it: or at least they tell me so. I wonder if that kind of writing is really worthwhile?"

At the back of MDH's mind for some years had been the problem of how to interest the general public in history and how she herself might write popular fiction, perhaps in the form of plays. MDH secretly harboured hopes that she could become a popular writer, respected by the general public, not just the serious and academic.

Since the book is primarily a list of names and there is an excellent index of names and places, recently, just for fun, I looked up my maiden name of Box in the Dugdale publication. To my surprise and delight, six people of that surname were mentioned and I believe that with the growing interest in family history, mediaeval registers such as these will become much consulted in the future.

IMMINENT DEMOLITION OF MEDIAEVAL STREETS IN COVENTRY

In late 1935 MDH knew that most of the picturesque narrow streets in Coventry, such as Little Butcher Row, were soon to be demolished. There were many in Coventry who disliked the dilapidated streets and plans made to replace them with wide thoroughfares, suitable for motor traffic, gained much approval in some quarters.

In mid 2001 I spoke with William Wilson, a Coventry resident for much of his life, former Labour MP for Coventry and ex-member of numerous councils. William Wilson said that as a young man in Coventry he felt ashamed of the run-down state of the Butcher Row area and he was delighted when demolition work actually began. I dare say many in Coventry felt the same, but how MDH's heart must have ached at the close of 1935.

"STAB THE LITTLE ROMAN REPTILE"

In November 1935, as if MDH did not have enough to do what with further work on the Guild Register, giving lectures and numerous other things, she acted the part of Ftatateeta in "Caesar and Cleopatra" by George Bernard Shaw. This meant there were numerous rehearsals to be fitted into her already overcrowded schedule. R.G. Slater recalled that at one rehearsal MDH achieved some quite amazing cruelty in her voice. Perhaps she achieved this by recalling all the historical vandals she had ever known!

"With all the vigour of which she is capable, Dor hisses out "Stab the little Roman reptile. Spit him with your sword" and with a quite amazing cruelty and abandon, "Why did you not stab him. There was time."

Those who know the play will recall that at the end of Act 1V Ftatateeta is found dead on the altar of Ra, with her throat cut; and that this is a most dramatic moment in the play. The part of Ftatateeta was certainly one in which she could demonstrate her great acting ability and after performances it took MDH some time to wash off the blood.

PERSONAL RECOLLECTIONS FROM RONALD SLATER

For a lively picture of MDH's life in the 1930s I am much indebted to *"A Memoir of Dor"*, written by one of her young friends, Ronald Slater, in India in 1937. By including a number of her conversations, he managed to convey a vivid picture of her. I have already quoted a number of extracts from his memoir, but it seems appropriate to close this chapter with a few revealing, often amusing, quotations from MDH's own lips.

I am reading for the first time the Iliad, Butler's, and enjoying it far more than a pacifist ought.

****

I saw yesterday that the tomb of Anne of Warwick's little son has turned up at

Sherrif Hutton in Yorkshire...seeing as I believe I was Anne of Warwick in a former life, everything about Richard the Third thrills me to the marrow of my childish self.

****

Present day conditions ..reveal a lop-sided world arranged for a) people of a certain standard of wealth and education b) mainly for men.

****

(Regarding a meeting with a famous literary critic and Cambridge University teacher)

I got on quite well with Mr Leavis. We fought of course, but with the utmost aimiability. and when I wished him goodbye he said "I am very pleased to have met you." Just as if he had come from Chicago and I was friend from California.

****

(of a beggar who often used to knock at her door)

My poor friend used to come almost daily. His gift of blarney was unique but he got terribly on my nerves. I couldn't get an afternoon nap for listening for his unwelcome ring. At last he got into trouble with the police and they retired him to the workhouse.. He wasn't doing any particular harm ... except ruining me and perhaps tippling.

****

I feel my own unworthiness. I ought to be walking about with a dust cart or playing about about in the sewers for four hours four days a week, instead of sitting at my ease editing Guild books and chatting and smoking and being frivolous... People want making over and over again and making different. I want making different, lots braver.

****

I had so many flowers that I gave the very old lady some next door, the body who objects to my noisy parties and knows whether all the people in Gaveston Road are gentry or not, and appreciates the cut of their clothes. Perhaps she won't be so hard on me now.

****

(After seeing the play in London "Richard of Bordeaux" starring John Gielgud)

Well may he be the divine Ellen's great nephew. He had a way of holding himself in, even when he was in a passion, that was marvellous.

****

It was all very nice at Wells till just before the end, when I came a cropper and lost my temper which is bad. A bad habit. Never mind. I saw the Cathedral through branches of cedars from my bedroom window.

****

(After a young male friend had explained who the All Blacks were)

Ah now I see. I seem to read and read and know nothing and here you are a perfect encyclopaedia. Eh what a stupid creature I am.

****

(To Philip Styles)

You know some day when "The Waters of Forgetfulness" gets put on at a London Theatre ....(you were a naughty darling in that charade) ...Well as I was saying when "The Beer of Remembrance" gets put on a London Theatre and I get oceans of money, I shall pack a toothbrush and nightie and start and see the world.

****

(about a scholarly friend she met in the library)

He is so eminently bullyable. It's bad for me I know. He excites my passion for tyranny.

****

Monks I have never loved. Twenty four of them wrapped up in themselves and saying prayers to themselves in an immense Çathedral with a great wall all around them, when people outside were struggling and starving and fighting and dying and getting drunk and going to the bad. No, no, St Francis for me...

****

Finally, the following extract from a letter MDH wrote to Robin Chapman (on January 1st 1936) paints a wonderful picture of a truly fun-loving, charismatic figure as she enjoyed Boxing Day 1935.

I had a jolly Boxing Day at the Styleses. Philip began by imitating a WEA student of his who speaks as if 40 plum stones were in his mouth and we all began to rock with laughing and continued so to rock until midnight. When you once begin to be silly like that, everything sets you off. It is very childish but great fun. We played a little bridge in between the laughing; but as Philip never will lead trumps, even if he has 5 honours, he and I did not come off very well. My play was not anything to boast of either. Then Mrs Styles began to wag her head and put out her tongue like a Chinese mandarin figure and that absolutely finished us; we were exhausted and could only wipe our streaming eyes and clutch our aching sides.

7. 1936 AND AFTERWARDS

DEMOLITION IN COVENTRY IN JANUARY 1936

On January 1st 1936 a number of mediaeval streets, which had been in existence in Coventry for around 500 years, were officially closed, and demolition began. I can only begin to imagine what Mary Dormer Harris felt about this. Although she had known for several years what was planned, she must have experienced a great sense of failure in that she and others had been unsuccessful in trying to convince the authorities that the old city centre had a modern future.

Even today many historians are appalled by the massive destruction of so many half-timbered properties and interesting old cellars, when countless archaeological treasures were obliterated before anyone had a chance to assess them properly. In 1936, antiquary John B. Shelton, of Little Park Street, Coventry, did his best to

TWO PHOTOGRAPHS OF MEDIAEVAL BUILDINGS IN COVENTRY, SHORTLY BEFORE THEY WERE DEMOLISHED, ARE PRESERVED IN THE COVENTRY CITY GUILD COLLECTION, IN COVENTRY CITY ARCHIVES.
This late 1935 photograph shows 17A Butcher Row, the premises of Jacob's House-furnishers, with a row of old chimney pots outside, no doubt removed from its own chimney stacks or nearby premises.

ON NEW YEAR'S DAY 1936 BUTCHER ROW WAS OFFICIALLY CLOSED AND IN THE MONTHS THAT FOLLOWED, MUCH OF COVENTRY'S MEDIAEVAL TOWN CENTRE WAS SWEPT AWAY BY GANGS OF DEMOLITION MEN. The half-timbered building, pictured in the previous photograph, is one of the few still more or less intact in this desolate and depressing scene.

record as much as possible, as excavations for new buildings followed demolitions, but it was a huge task.

In his recent book "The City of Coventry, Images from the Past," David McGrory, a modern historian of Coventry, called the demolition of Butcher Row and the other picturesque streets *"barbarous vandalism"* I must say I agree with him, although many people in 1936 seem to have felt it was necessary.

DEATH OF KING GEORGE V

In the early weeks of 1936 many other things were changing too. King George V died on 21st January and Edward the VIII became King. MDH and Philip Styles went to hear the new king proclaimed outside Leamington Town Hall, but as she told another young friend, Robin Chapman, in a letter, their plans went somewhat awry.

"Philip insisted I should go down with him to hear the new king proclaimed (I suppose being history people we like that sort of thing). It was a bit early, about 20 to 10 a.m. but anyway I went instead of staying at home and hearing it on the

wireless from St James's Palace. And it wasn't at 10 after all at Leamington. There was an interregnum of two hours. King E. VIII was proclaimed at 12 o'clock in Leamington instead of 9.55. Anyway we went to the Cadena, where Philip very kindly treated me to some rather weak coffee, and all the time there was a wireless going with guns and voices, so we heard something."

THE NEW COVENTRY CITY GUILD

On Tuesday February 25th 1936, at 7 pm in St Mary's Hall, the inaugural meeting of the new Coventry City Guild took place. Lesser people might have been tempted to stay away from the city, but it seems that MDH, despite all, felt that her heart was in Coventry. When making her way to the meeting she was doubtless aware of the demolition going on nearby. To raze dozens of properties so that the new Trinity Street and a large department store for Owen and Owen could be built, seemed dreadful for much of her life's work had been bound up in those mediaeval buildings. However she was a realist and in the severe economic depression of the 1930s, even she may have wondered whether urgent modern needs should take precedence and whether large new shops would bring increased prosperity to the city.

Before the new constitution and rules of the new guild were discussed, Mr Serge Chermayeff gave an address about modern buildings and afterwards MDH seconded the vote of thanks given by Malcolm Pridmore.

In the discussion which followed later, MDH addressed the meeting. She described herself as one of the few survivors of the old Guild and said,

"We have been reminded that it is wrong to turn our attention too much to the past. I agree that we must try and work for the future. ... Much beauty still remains, and the Guild must preserve the beauties of nature while making our modern buildings and planning worthy of the past."

In the course of the evening, a new committee was elected and it was no surprise to find MDH's name on it, alongside that of Dr Walter Brazil, Angela Brazil and R.T. Howard, the Provost of Coventry.

"THE BRIDGE"

Following several letters in 1935, the Weston-Super-Mare Dramatic Society chose to perform MDH's play in a Drama League in early 1936. Their request pleased her enormously.

When the Judge's comments came they were very complimentary and in the competition the performance of "The Bridge" was placed joint second. The Adjudicator had written,

"The treatment of this beautiful little play was well developed, and consequently it established itself in the favour of the audience. ...The story is symbolic - of travellers after death crossing the Styx on their way to the abiding place of the blest. There is something intangibly grave and mystical, something of the lonely Celtic Twilight, about this lovely fancy."

Sadly MDH did not live to read these comments. How she would have relished the sentences in the last paragraph of the Adjudicator's comments.

"...The author showed a beautiful thought...(It is) *a very sincere and beautiful play which must command our respect."*

MONDAY MARCH 2ND 1936

As usual this was a packed day for Mary Dormer Harris and she spent it much as she had spent many others.

In the morning she went to Warwick with Philip Styles. They spent nearly three hours going round the Shire Hall, where they were given a conducted tour by Mr W.A.Sutton (Clerk to the Records Committee) and the Infantry Record Office in St John's House, being conducted round by Colonel Hughes (the Infantry Record Officer). The visits were in preparation for another article by MDH for the "Coventry Herald". She and Philip Styles then had lunch together in Leamington and they parted at around 3 o'clock.

She probably had a rest in the afternoon, as was usual, and in the evening she went to a meeting of the Workers' Educational Association at which Philip Styles was speaking. She was a Vice President of the Association and for many years she had taken a great interest in it.

After the meeting, which was held in central Leamington, she walked away accompanied by a friend. Shortly after parting from her friend, she attempted to cross Rugby Road on her own. She never reached the other side for she was struck by a car and died almost immediately.

TUESDAY MARCH 3RD 1936

As she carried no handbag and had no identification on her person, her body was not indentified until the following morning. Few then had private telephones and most of her friends knew nothing until they read the newspaper reports. Later on the Tuesday the news broke and the 'Last Edition' of the "Midland Daily Telegraph" of Tuesday March 3rd had a prominent section of the front page devoted to her death. Four head-lines preceded the article.

TRAGIC DEATH OF MISS DORMER HARRIS

Knocked Down by Car at Leamington

EMINENT WARWICKSHIRE HISTORIAN

TRANSCRIBED THE COVENTRY LEET BOOK

"It is with regret that we announce the death of Miss Mary Dormer Harris, the eminent Warwickshire historian, in tragic circumstances.

About ten o'clock last night Miss Dormer Harris, who resided in Gaveston Road, Leamington, was crossing the road near her home when she was knocked down by a motor car and fatally injured. She was taken to the Warneford Hospital immediately, but was found to be dead on arrival."

A long article, full of biographical details gleaned from their files, then followed. All the other local newspapers had similar coverage spread over the next few days and later some national papers carried obituaries.

THE INQUEST

The inquest was held on Wednesday March 4th at Leamington Police Station in High Street. Both the Coroner Mr E.F. Hadow and the Jury paid tribute to the work Miss Dormer Harris had done.

Miss Margaret Elizabeth Dormer of Yew Tree Cottage, Rowington gave evidence of identification. She also added that her cousin was very short-sighted and slightly absent-minded and would often be thinking about something else when walking along.

STATEMENT BY AN EYE-WITNESS

Mr Harry Castle, of 5 Milverton Crescent West said that at about 9.55 p.m. he was walking towards Rugby Road and when he was about eight yards from it, he saw a woman crossing Rugby Road diagonally. He heard a car coming from Warwick, but could not see it. The woman went over the crown of the road, seemed to hestitate and then hurried on. He went on,

"By the time I had reached Rugby Road, the car was going over Gaveston Road and the next thing I saw was the old lady attempting to cross the road, going rather quickly with her head down.. I then heard a loud report and the car stopped immediately. I have never seen a car stop so quickly. The body of the woman was lying just clear of the front wheels. I got some men to lift the car up while I dragged her out and the ambulance was summoned. I must congratulate the ambulance on the speed with which they got there. I dragged her to the side of the road and propped her head up, while Dr Hayward also gave assistance. The car was coming at a very reasonable speed, but where the lady was struck it was very dark."

The witness said he was of the opinion that Miss Dormer Harris had heard the car but did not see it.

THE CAR WAS DRIVEN BY A LOCAL WOMAN

The car was being driven by Dr Lilian Anne Hayward of 65 Northumberland Road, and she had two passengers, Miss Elizabeth Walker Anderson, housekeeper at the County Mental Hospital, and Miss Paulette Maynard of Weald, Harrow.

Dr Hayward said *"My speed was 20 to 25 mph at most. Just past the entrance to Gaveston Road, I saw quite suddenly an obstacle about a yard from the off-side mudguard. I saw a black object; I didn't know if it was a man or a woman; or what it was. I just had a feeling of danger and that I had to stop. I pulled up very quickly but the car went gently over the object in front."*

After describing how the car had been tilted to allow the person to be extricated the driver went on,

"I tried Miss Dormer Harris's pulse but could not feel it. I believe she was dead before the ambulance arrived."

ACCIDENTAL DEATH

Medical evidence given by Dr B.S. Jones showed that death was due to multiple injuries and a fractured skull. He said that death would have been practically instantaneous.

D.O. Toone (Coroner's Officer) said it was a well-known fact that Miss Dormer Harris invariably walked with her head down. When addressing the Jury the Coroner paid tribute to Miss Dormer Harris and said that from the evidence he thought the car was being driven reasonably, at a speed of perhaps 15 mph in view of the short distance in which the driver pulled up.

The Jury returned a verdict of Accidental Death and exonerated the driver of all blame. The Foreman, Mr T.J. Kennard, said he was sure, regarding Miss Dormer Harris, that it was a case in which the good she had done would not be interred with her bones.

Sympathy was expressed for the relatives, and the Coroner also sympathized with Dr Hayward who had had a most upsetting experience.

WAS THERE A MEDICAL CAUSE?

Obviously there is no means of telling for sure, but with the benefit of hindsight and the ability to understand the wider picture, it seems to me that there may well have been a medical cause for the fact that MDH apparently heard the car but did not see it.

We know that her maternal grandmother had gone blind and that she herself had had trouble with her eyesight almost thirty years previously. I am far from being a medical expert, but from the little I do know I think it is quite possible that she suffered from glaucoma or some other disease which caused the loss of peripheral vision.

If she habitually walked with her head down, it may well have been that she needed to concentrate on the ground immediately in front of where she was walking. She may have been engrossed in things as she walked around, but she was certainly not stupid and would not have allowed her concentration to lapse when crossing a road.

If she did have glaucoma causing restricted vision, she might not have been aware of just how vulnerable she had become.

"TO CEASE UPON THE MIDNIGHT WITH NO PAIN"

There is plenty of evidence in her later works to show that MDH had given considerable thought to death. The last lines of her play "St George and the Dragon" concern death, and in the concluding paragraph of an article "Uncle Jasper", she described the death of her much-loved relation. The article ends with the sentence,

"He had died, as we all wish to die - 'to cease upon the midnight with no pain'."

When MDH died, at the side of the road, just yards from her home, I like to think that these words from "Ode to Nightingale" applied to her as well. She was fond of quoting her beloved Keats and, although it was two hours before midnight and she might have suffered for a few seconds, it was near enough for the words to have been appropriate.

SOME FINE OBITUARIES

Of all the obituaries carried in Midlands newspapers perhaps the finest tribute paid was contained in an un-named paper dated Wednesday March 4th. All I have is a small cutting, but it appears to be a leading article which begins with this paragraph.

"Philanthropy has its myriad forms. It does not consist merely of giving, from the bounty of the giver's substance, to those less well endowed with the necessities of life.... Those who give freely of their knowledge, time, ability and skill to the service of their fellows are philanthropists in at least as real a sense as those who gain that honoured distinction in its more material significance. Miss Mary Dormer Harris was a true philanthropist. She devoted her life to the study of the ancient lore of the Coventry and the Warwickshire she loved, and gave freely of the knowledge she gained by many years of unremitting toil."

The Provost of Coventry paid her a great tribute in a letter dated March 4th 1936, which he sent to local newspapers.

"On behalf of the Cathedral Church I desire to express a deep sense of bereavement on hearing the sad news of the death of Miss Dormer Harris. We have lost a very great woman from our midst..."

The Provost then referred to her wide knowledge, affectionate interest in almost every corner and stone of the Cathedral and her infectious gaiety and humour.

A RESOLUTION PASSED IN A CORPORATION COMMITTEE

When the Amenities Committee of Coventry Corporation met on March 21st 1936 a resolution was passed concerning her death.

"...the Amenities Committee express their sorrow at the death of Miss Mary Dormer Harris and their grateful appreciation of the valuable services she rendered to the City of Coventry of so many years in the study and interpretation of its ancient records, and in their recognition of the wide scholarship and the literary skill with which she accomplished a task which has gained for her a pre-eminent place amongst the historians of Coventry."

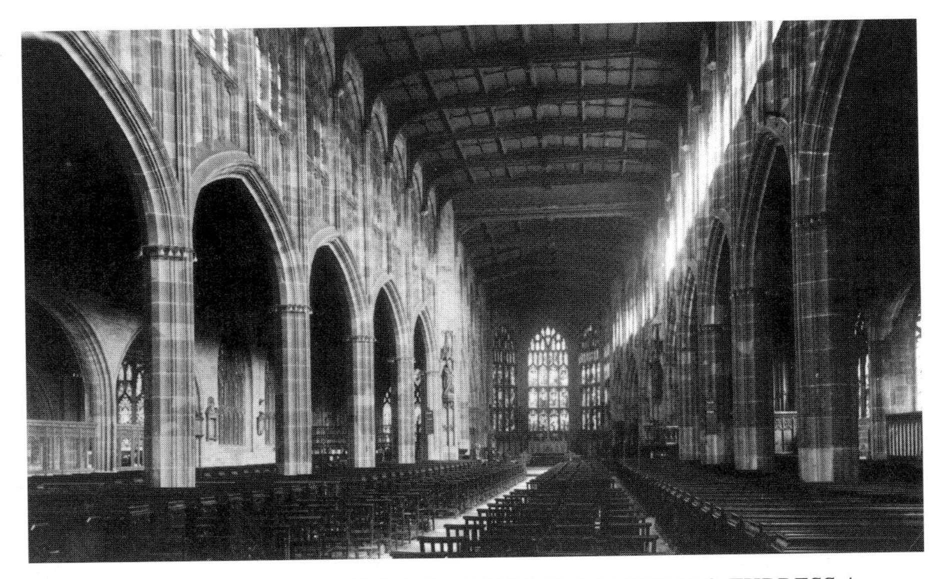

"ON BEHALF OF THE CATHEDRAL CHURCH I DESIRE TO EXPRESS A DEEP SENSE OF BEREAVEMENT ON HEARING THE SAD NEWS OF THE DEATH OF MISS DORMER HARRIS." So said R.T. Howard, the Provost of Coventry, on March 4th 1936. This 1936 view of the interior of St Michael's Cathedral serves to remind us of the vast knowledge which Mary Dormer Harris had of this beautiful building. "The first time I had the privilege of meeting her was as a member of a party she was taking round the Cathedral. I was immediately captured by her affectionate interest in almost every corner and stone of the building," the Provost said.

AN OBITUARY FROM OXFORD

The brief compliment which might have pleased Mary Dormer Harris the most was one made at the end of her obituary in "The Brown Book" of 1936 at her Oxford College, Lady Margaret Hall.

G.E.E. (perhaps Gertrude Elizabeth Edwards who had been a student at the same time as MDH) wrote,

"...and Oxford may be proud of yet another scholar who has helped to build Jerusalem."

THE FUNERAL

The funeral took place at noon on Friday 6th March. The service was held in St Mark's Church, close to her home at Gaveston Road and interment was in the same grave as her mother at Milverton Cemetery. There were nearly one hundred people in the church for the service and over sixty floral tributes were received.

Left: THE MAYOR AND MAYORESS OF COVENTRY, ALDERMAN AND MRS PAYNE, ARRIVING AT THE FUNERAL OF MARY DORMER HARRIS IN ST MARK'S CHURCH, LEAMINGTON SPA ON 6TH MARCH 1936.
Right: MISS DOORLY, HEADMISTRESS OF THE KING'S HIGH SCHOOL WARWICK, SENT A WREATH TO THE FUNERAL OF MARY DORMER HARRIS WITH A MOST APT MESSAGE ON THE ACCOMPANYING CARD "IN ADMIRATION AND SORROW". Eleanor Doorly, pictured here in the garden of Landor House, was herself a highly - successful writer of books for children.

Amongst the mourners were eight of her numerous cousins and various close friends including Florence Hayllar and Mary Whitefoord. Prominent in the congregation were the Mayor and Mayoress of Coventry and there was a civic wreath which bore the message *"From the Corporation of Coventry in grateful remembrance of many acts of service to their City."* The Editor and Manager of the 'Midland Daily Telegraph' was there as was Mr A. Stewart McMillan, Editor of the 'Coventry Herald'.

Philip Styles was of course at the funeral, as was the woman he married some years later, Dorothy Sutcliffe, who represented Birmingham University. Philip Chatwin represented the Birmingham Archaeological Society; Mr F. Quaintance, the Leamington Branch of the League of Nations Union; Mr F.C. Wellstood and Mr W.F. Carter, the Dugdale Society; Mr G.C.W. Large, the Drapers' Company of

Coventry; Miss E. Round, Students' Historical Fellowship of Birmingham University; Mr and Mrs..A C. Bunch, the Leamington Literary Society; Councillor C.W. Gardner, Mr Rueben Wright and Mrs Bragg, the Leamington Labour Party; Mr and Mrs F.S. Webb, Mr H.G. Matthews, Mr and Mrs Arnold Thornton and Mrs A.T. Lees, the Leamington and Warwick Dramatic Study Club; and Mr A.H. Gardner, Mrs Mitchell Smith and Mr G.F.B. Pierson, the Coventry City Guild.

Various other people were represented. Miss Doorly, Headmistress of King's High School was represented by the School Secretary, Miss R. Oldham, who was a distant relation of Mary Dormer Harris. Herself a popular writer of children's books, Miss Doorly sent a wreath with a brief, but appropriate message. *"With admiration and sorrow from Eleanor Doorly"*. Mrs Ellen Dykes, who had been treasurer of the Suffragists' Society over thirty years previously was present, as was her daughter Marion.

The funeral service was conducted by Rev. G.H.K. Pedley, Vicar of All Saints Emscote, assisted by Rev. W.L.Gutch, who was the husband of Phyllis (née Dormer) a cousin of Mary Dormer Harris. Mr George Kennett was the organist.

Two of MDH's young friends were abroad and missed the funeral. Ronald Slater was in India and Robin Chapman in South Africa and when both received letters from their relations, they were deeply shocked and saddened by the news.

THE GRAVE AT MILVERTON CEMETERY

Mrs Harris had been buried in the cemetery in Old Milverton Lane, Leamington Spa and an inscription had been placed on two sides of the kerb stone. "MARY, WIDOW OF THOMAS HARRIS OF STONELEIGH / DIED MAY 15TH 1923 AGED 89." After the death of Mary Dormer Harris, an inscription "AND HER DAUGHTER MARY DORMER HARRIS, HISTORIAN AND ARCHAEOLOGIST. BORN AT STONELEIGH AUG. 11TH 1867. DIED MARCH 2ND 1936." was added to the other long side, the text "THE GREATEST OF THESE IS LOVE" being inscribed on the remaining short side.

THE WILL

There must have been some who had a pleasant surprise when MDH's will was examined, It had been made four years previously on 4th February 1932 and the executors were her friend Miss Mary Whitefoord and Mr J.E. Linford, the Manager of the Leamington branch of the Midland Bank, who each had legacies for their trouble.

Some of MDH's relations were the main beneficiaries, but there were also a number of small legacies to the young people who had helped to make her last years so lively and enjoyable. Philip Styles was left £25, Clifford Sleath £50 and Ronald Slater £25. The City of Coventry was not forgotten and the Gulson Library was left such books *"as the Librarian of that Library may select."* Ronald Slater was left the rest of the books.

For some years MDH had been helping with orthopaedic cases via the Rotary Club, and the fact that one Louisa Kimberley Price of Headingley, Leeds, had a mini-trust fund set up for her, suggested that she was ill or disabled. After her death the money was to benefit Florence Moss of Brampton House, Newcastle, Staffordshire.

Perhaps the most interesting legacy was that of the royalties of her books to her old college friend Florence Hayllar who also had a legacy of £100.

Several cousins had legacies and family possessions left to them, and the cousins who benefited most were John Garner Dormer, Margaret Elizabeth Dormer, James Garrard Dormer, Elin Mary Gutch (née Dormer) and Sarah Phyllis Gutch (née Dormer).

Around six weeks later, when Probate of the will was granted, the gross amount of the estate was declared to be just over £4,087 and the net amount £3,404. (In 1936 a new semi-detached house in the Leamington area cost around £500, so some idea of today's equivalent can be gained.) However by no standards could MDH have been termed a wealthy woman and it would appear that both she and her mother had lived fairly economically on small fixed incomes, which it was possible to do before the Second World War.

UNFINISHED BUSINESS

When a busy writer dies suddenly, a large amount of unfinished business is often left behind, and in the case of MDH much of this incomplete work concerned further transcriptions connected with the Register of the Guild of Holy Trinity. A letter from F.C. Wellstood, Director of the Shakespeare Birthplace Trust and Hon. Secretary and General Editor of the Dugdale Society to Mr Smith, Town Clerk of Coventry, made the situation very clear. The letter was dated 25th March 1936.

After thanking Mr Smith for allowing another MS to be deposited at Shakespeare's Birthplace, he explained that it might be necessary for the Register itself to be deposited in Stratford for a short time. Mr Wellstood then referred to MDH.

"I hope that it may be possible for me to complete the text of the volume towards which she had done so much at the time of her death, but of course there is no one alive who could supply the historical introduction as she would have done it.

...Her death is certainly a great loss to Coventry and to the cause of mediaeval scholarship generally."

A SENSE OF SHOCK

As the days and weeks passed it became clear that the initial sense of shock felt by her friends was still present. A memorial to Mary Dormer Harris was called for, and in the months after her death there were letters to local newspapers with ideas. It was generally felt that a Memorial Fund would be a good idea, but the suggestions as to what could be done with the money ranged from a scholarship to send a poor

F.C. WELLSTOOD, SECRETARY AND LIBRARIAN OF THE SHAKESPEARE BIRTHPLACE TRUST FROM 1910 TO 1942, PHOTOGRAPHED IN 1935. He was also Honorary Secretary and General Editor of the Dugdale Society and he had a great respect for Mary Dormer Harris.

Coventry boy to university to setting up a home for impoverished gentle-ladies. In the end it took two years to get a subscription fund up and running, and it was decided that the fund should be used to grant bursaries to needy students in the mid Warwickshire area.

THE CITY OF COVENTRY NEEDED AN ARCHIVIST

The Town Clerk of Coventry knew only too well that the death of MDH had caused many problems. The city now had no one to read its old documents and soon it was thought urgent for a professional archivist to be engaged. Work which she had done, largely free of charge except for an occasional honorarium, was now to cost the Corporation a salary of £260, rising to £300 p.a. if a man was appointed, or £200 a year, rising to £250, for a woman. Levi Fox (later Director of the Shakespeare Birthplace Trust) was appointed as archivist and took up his duties on 1st March 1938.

TWO POSTHUMOUS BOOKS

The Coventry City Guild decided to publish a memorial volume of a collection of Mary Dormer Harris's newspaper articles and five hundred copies were printed in 1937. (See Part Two of this book). The book began with several tributes and one by Florence Hayllar perhaps summed up MDH's character better than any.

"...In Molly's company all the things that count - joke and merriment, poetry, the lives of people, discussions on the problems of life and being - were enhanced, lighted up, freshly coloured. One was always so glad when she was coming and so sorry when she went away."

Florence Hayllar took her duties as literary executor very seriously and a couple of years afterwards she edited a book of MDH's plays and essays. The book was printed in Leamington at the Courier Press and it contained the full text of "Waters of Forgetfulness", "The Bridge" and "St George and the Dragon."

IN 1937 COVENTRY CITY GUILD PUBLISHED A POSTHUMOUS BOOK OF ARTICLES BY MARY DORMER HARRIS. The frontispiece to that book was a photograph similar to this one, taken in the last few years of her life.

8. THE MEMORIAL BURSARY AND OTHER MEMORIALS

LAUNCH OF THE MEMORIAL BURSARY FUND

At a public meeting held in Leamington Town Hall on February 1st 1938 it was decided to appeal for funds to endow a Bursary in memory of Mary Dormer Harris. The well-attended meeting was chaired by the Mayor of Leamington, Alderman Charles Davis, who said that he and Miss Harris were old friends as they were two of the remaining eight original members of the Dramatic Study Club. He paid her the great compliment of saying that she was *"always a very happy person."*

When he spoke, Philip Chatwin said *"...it is to be hoped that future generations will realise that by means of this memorial, how highly this little lady was appreciated by her friends and admirers."*

A large committee of thirty people was appointed to frame a scheme and to appoint an Executive committee, with powers to co-opt. By 25th February, an Executive Committee of twelve members had been elected with Philip Chatwin as Chairman, H.M. Jenkins as Treasurer and Gertrude Bark and Phyllis Hicks as Joint Secretaries. A leaflet was prepared and printed which ended,

"We confidently rely upon all those who knew, directly or indirectly, the value of Miss Dormer Harris's work, to provide a memorial worthy of her place in the hearts of all Warwickshire people."

It was hoped that the fund would raise a thousand pounds and in the beginning some large donations were made. Mr and Mrs J. Alfred Hill gave £50 and five people, including Mary Whitefoord, gave £25. A number of other people gave what they could afford and there were a large number of donations of five shillings. Eleanor Doorly, Headmistress of the King's High School in Warwick, sent five shillings and an explanatory note to Phyllis Hicks. *"I am sorry it isn't more, but I have my own scholarships to see to here."*

Almost all of Mary Dormer Harris's relations sent donations and cousin Edith Garner (Mrs Lee-Hankey) of Hampstead, was amongst those who sent letters of encouragement with their cheque. Another cousin, William Hurlstone Hortin of Tolleshunt D'Arcy, Malden, Essex, sent a note with his donation saying that Mrs Harris had been his godmother.

There were quite a number of contributions from individuals in Coventry, but nothing was received from any of the Brazil family, so perhaps talk of the rivalry between the two writers had been true after all. However the prominent Coventry antiquary John Bailey Shelton, of Little Park Street, sent a donation and it was likely that he and MDH knew each other well. Other notables who donated were Sir Alfred Herbert, Colonel Wyley and Sir W.F.S.Dugdale.

The money continued to come in steadily for some months, but it became evident that the target of a thousand pounds would not be reached. After twelve months, around 150 donations had been received, including some from abroad, and a sum of just under £500 was raised.

The money donated was invested and the interest used to pay the bursary. In the early years, applications (no more than one per school) were made solely by the head-teachers of the secondary schools and the applications were considered at an annual meeting of the Trustees. The first payment was made in July 1939.

In later years, more schools in the Mid Warwickshire area were invited to send in applications and the students themselves filled in the forms. However, the applications are still endorsed by a letter from the headteachers who send in the forms.

Complete lists of Trustees and Bursary winners are be found in the Appendix. That this Memorial Fund has continued to function well for sixty-four years is a matter for some pride because at times the difficulties have been immense. The first dedicated band of Trustees gave unstintingly of their time and effort. From time to time, as inflation whittled away the value of the capital, further donations and bequests, largely from Trustees or previous Trustees, redressed the balance.

The Trust was entered in the Register of Charities in 1964 (under the Charities Act of 1960) and was subsequently updated in 1991 under new legislation and given its Registration Number by the Charity Commissioners (528762).

In retrospect, it was a wise choice to endow a bursary fund for students with money collected in memory of Mary Dormer Harris, for the need for such a fund has increased, rather than decreased, with the passage of time.

THOSE DEDICATED FRIENDS

A few friends of MDH did so much to help the Bursary Fund for so long that this book would be incomplete without some special mention of them.

Philip Chatwin was the first Chairman of the Memorial Bursary Trust and both he and his wife Cecily did all they could to help the fund. Many of the annual meetings of the Trustees were held at their house 26 Binswood Avenue, and as the Diocesan Architect, a keen archaeologist and prominent Coventry Guild Committee member, Philip did much to keep alive the memory of MDH.

Herbert M. Jenkins who lived with his mother at 46 Rugby Road, Leamington first met MDH after the First World War when he admired her work and found that she lived nearby. They went on long walks together in the 1920s and later MDH often visited his home, jokingly referring to him once as *"a walking encyclopaedia of the Warwickshire families."* Sharing a great interest in the Dugdale Society, Herbert Jenkins gave a lecture in Leamington in 1931 on "Dr Thomas's edition of Sir William Dugdale's Antiquaries of Warwickshire" and this was printed by the Dugdale Society as 'Occasional Papers Number 3'. H.M. Jenkins worked as a bank official and he was Treasurer of the Memorial Trust for over 33 years, remaining so

Left: HERBERT M. JENKINS WAS THE FIRST TREASURER OF THE MARY DORMER HARRIS MEMORIAL BURSARY TRUST. He remained in the post for over 33 years. After he moved to Hampshire, he still returned to Leamington occasionally and he is seen here in 1977 at the launch of "The Leamington We Used to Know" a book compiled by the Leamington Literary Society, which he had supported for many years.
Right: GERTRUDE BARK, PICTURED HERE AROUND 1970, WAS A TRUSTEE OF THE MARY DORMER HARRIS MEMORIAL BURSARY FOR OVER FIFTY YEARS. For much of that time she was Secretary.

even after he moved to Hampshire. He was also a keen member of the Leamington Literary Society and contributed to the several books of Leamington history, edited by Kathleen Hanks, in the 1970s and early 1980s.

Gertrude Bark was the first Secretary of the Trust (the first few years jointly with Phyllis Hicks) and she became the longest serving of the Trustees having served for over fifty years by the time of her death in 1990. She first met MDH in 1924 when, newly married, she moved to Leamington from Lancashire. Many Trustees' Meetings were held in her house 147 Leam Terrace, Leamington and she was instrumental in organising a "Mary Dormer Harris Centenary" on October 14th 1967. She had shared MDH's love of Shakespeare and drama and was a fine musician. Today Gertrude Bark also has a Memorial Bursary bearing her name which is awarded to students of music, literature or drama in the Warwick and Leamington area.

Phyllis Hicks was Secretary (jointly with Gertrude Bark) until her own tragic death at the early age of 46 in 1952. Her mother had died at an early age and Phyllis gave up a college course to return to Leamington to care for her father who was Editor of the "Leamington Spa Courier". She had a promising career as a journalist and drama critic, writing for her father's paper and many other publications. Phyllis developed diabetes and eventually both she and her father went blind and died within a few months of each other. Edward and Phyllis Hicks lived at 39 Gaveston Road, not far from MDH.

It is interesting to note that Phyllis Hicks also became a friend of Florence Hayllar, MDH's college friend and literary executor. When Miss Hayllar died in 1942 she left a number of religous items to friends including a "Russian Ikon" to Phyllis Hicks. It may well have been that Florence Hayllar accompanied MDH and Phyllis when they travelled to France and Germany for holidays.

Personally I have a very soft spot for Phyllis Hicks for in 1942 (at the annual meeting of the Bursary Trustees) she was asked to undertake the writing of a biography of MDH. Although she began to amass material, this was never completed and in some ways I feel I am concluding business which she started. In the course of my research I have been using many of the letters and notes which were filed away by her. After Phyllis's death, Gertrude Bark continued to gather these archives connected with MDH, adding many notes of her own.

Some years after Phyllis's death, her younger sister Mary Elliott (née Hicks) became a Trustee and she served faithfully for many years, even travelling from her home in Leicestershire for the annual meetings.

Philip Styles was not a member of the original committee but he became one later and on the death of Philip Chatwin he was elected Chairman. Philip had been a special friend of MDH in the 1930s and both had helped the other a huge amount. He was a pupil at the Leamington College for Boys from 1914-1923 and had then studied history at Worcester College, Oxford. Although he lived at 69 Greatheed Road, just round the corner from Gaveston Road, Philip had probably come into contact with MDH at the Leamington Literary Society or the Loft Theatre. For many years he was a Reader in History at the University of Birmingham. When the Centenary of MDH was held in the Urquhart Hall, Leamington in 1967, Philip Styles was one of the main contributors and he and H.G. Matthews had a public conversation as part of the programme.

Another duo who deserve special mention are Rev. Ronald Slater writer of the excellent "Memoir of Dor," and his school-teacher sister Amy Nora Slater who was an Old Girl of King's High School, Warwick. Having had a deep respect for MDH, Ronald Slater was one of the first Trustees, but almost immediately, he had to return abroad. In 1941, his sister Nora became a Trustee in his place and she proved to be a huge asset. In July 1955, as Phyllis Hicks had been unable to complete a biography, Nora compiled a useful folder of information about MDH and for around forty-five years she was a very loyal Trustee. Ronald Slater died in 1989 and his sister in 1999 aged 100. Like other past trustees, both of them left money in their wills to the Memorial Bursary Trust, which was a cause close to their hearts.

Robin Chapman, who had been encouraged by MDH as a student and young teacher, held the office of Chairman for fourteen years, and Clifford Sleath took over the role of Treasurer in 1977, having been one of the original Trustees in 1938. Rev. Reg Osborn, Mrs Mitchell Smith, and many others who had been special friends of MDH served as Trustees.

THE MARY DORMER HARRIS CENTENARY EVENING IN 1967

The problem with Memorial Bursaries is that the person after whom the fund is named sometimes becomes forgotten and to avoid this a Centenary Evening was organised jointly by the Loft Theatre and the Bursary Trust. Philip Styles was then the Chairman of the Bursary Trust and Harold G. Baker, the Chairman of the Loft Theatre.

An enjoyable evening was had by a large number of those who had known MDH, or been Bursary winners, at the Urquart Hall in Leamington on 14th October 1967 and during the evening a collection was taken to enable a seat in the new Loft Theatre to be endowed in her name. The Loft Theatre was in the process of being rebuilt, following a fire, and for some years afterwards, the middle seat of the front row bore the name of Mary Dormer Harris.

IN OCTOBER 1967 A MARY DORMER HARRIS CENTENARY EVENING WAS HELD AT THE URQUART HALL IN LEAMINGTON SPA. Many of the those attending had known MDH personally and this photograph shows a section of the rapt audience.

THE SIXTIETH ANNIVERSARY OF THE FIRST AWARD MADE BY THE MEMORIAL BURSARY TRUST WAS MARKED BY A CELEBRATORY EVENING AT THE LOFT THEATRE IN LEAMINGTON SPA IN SEPTEMBER 1998. Rebecca Vick of Kineton High School and Adam Cox of King Edward VI School, Stratford-upon-Avon were presented with their awards in the course of the evening.

READING OF "THE WATERS OF FORGETFULNESS" 1994

On 10th May 1994 the Leamington Literary Society held a reading of the "Waters of Forgetfulness" in the Regent Hotel and after the meeting Angela Cameron, as Chairman of the Bursary Trustees, gave a short talk about MDH, inviting anyone who felt inclined to help, to volunteer. As a result of this, Graham Cooper, who had read the part of the king, said that he was interested and within months he had been invited to become a Trustee. He is now into his eighth year as a Trustee and he has been Secretary since 1997.

LITERARY LUNCH IN 1998 TO RAISE FUNDS

On 6th March 1998, a Literary Lunch at Claverdon Church Centre was organised by Bursary Trustee, Shirley Reading, the speakers being two former school-friends of hers, namely Pauline Harris, a highly-successful writer of romantic fiction, and myself as a fellow Trustee and the author of several local history books. That event raised £500 for the Bursary Fund and besides bringing welcome publicity, proved an enjoyable occasion for all concerned.

"AS SHE LIKED IT" 60TH ANNIVERSARY OF THE BURSARY TRUST IN 1998

In order to mark the 60th anniversary of the Memorial Bursary Trust an evening performance of suitable words and music was held at the Loft Theatre on 20th September 1998. The company included Ann Mulraine, Sue and Richard Moore, Amy and Jeremy Heynes, Ann Williams, Michael Rayns and Edward Pinner, with the music being provided by Gwen Thomas and Julian Harris. MDH's play "St George and the Dragon" was read and Victorian songs, such as "Home Sweet Home," performed.

ON 11TH AUGUST 2001 (THE 134TH ANNIVERSARY OF THE BIRTH OF MARY DORMER HARRIS) SIX OF THE CURRENT TRUSTEES OF THE MEMORIAL BURSARY GATHERED IN MILVERTON CEMETERY, LEAMINGTON SPA TO LAY FLOWERS ON HER RECENTLY RESTORED GRAVE. From left to right they are John Jenkins, Graham Cooper (Secretary), Angela Cameron (Former Chairman), Shirley Reading (Chairman), Syd Creed (Treasurer), and Jean Field.

RESTORATION OF THE GRAVE

In early 2001, the kerb-stone of the grave of Mary Dormer Harris and her mother was found to be in need of restoration and remedial work was carried out on the loose, moss-covered stones, by Raymond C. Pullin, a masonry consultant. The necessary work was done at the personal expense of the Trustees. On 11th August 2001, the 134th anniversary of the birth of MDH, six of the current Trustees gathered at the newly-restored grave, with floral tributes.

At present there are ten Trustees whose names will be found in the list in the Appendix and further investigation will show that one person has been a Trustee for far longer than anyone else and also that she had been a bursary winner some years previously. Caroline Haynes spoke for all the Trustees and Bursary winners when she made the following statement.

"MY INVOLVEMENT WITH THE MARY DORMER MEMORIAL BURSARY" BY CAROLINE HAYNES, THE LONGEST-SERVING OF THE PRESENT TRUSTEES

In 1968 I was invited to become a Trustee of the Memorial Bursary as it was felt that new blood was needed on the body of ageing Trustees. The reason that I was given this honour was that in 1960, when a pupil at the Kingsley School, Leamington Spa, I had been awarded money from the bursary. As a result I had become interested in the life of Mary Dormer Harris. Almost all the other Trustees serving in 1968 had been friends of Mary Dormer Harris and I felt it was a great privilege to join them.

It is because I have knowledge of both the giving and receiving of this bursary that I have been asked to write a few paragraphs for this book. When I was awarded a bursary at the age of eighteen it made a big difference to my life at a time when I was in need of help. Since 1968 I have been an ordinary Trustee, then Joint Honorary Secretary and later sole Secretary from 1985 to 1996, so I have knowledge of the great effort put in by all the Trustees which enables this award to keep going, even in times of inflation when the value of our capital is whittled away. That so many young students, including myself, have had assistance from the bursary fund is a great compliment to the loyalty and integrity of trustees past and present.

Mary Dormer Harris must have been an exceptional woman and a truly charismatic figure and thanks to all those who have helped by donating money or administering the Memorial Trust, she continues to inspire us today.

CAROLINE HAYNES, PICTURED AROUND THE TIME SHE WON THE BURSARY IN 1960.

9. LOOSE ENDS

COVENTRY

Many of the best-planned schemes in life come to nothing and several of Mary Dormer Harris most cherished dreams fell into this category. The Cathedral Church of St Michael, which was so dear to her heart, was destroyed by enemy action on 14th November 1940. Today, only the famous ruin remains, adjacent to the new Coventry Cathedral.

Her beloved Palace-Yard, after having being successfully repaired and refurbished, was completely destroyed by a single high-explosive bomb on the same night as the Cathedral. Within seconds much of the old house had become rubble. The Gulson Library, which had taken some of her own books, was also severely damaged by enemy action and many of the items in its care were lost.

Other ancient buildings were more fortunate. St Mary's Hall escaped serious damage, and although Ford's Hospital was hit by a bomb in October 1940, it was later restored to its former glory and re-opened in 1953.

When new Council houses were built in Tile Hill in the 1950s, one of the roads was named Dormer Harris Avenue to honour the memory of Mary Dormer Harris.

WHEN NEW HOUSES WERE BUILT IN TILE HILL, COVENTRY IN THE 1950s, ONE OF THE NEW ROADS WAS NAMED DORMER HARRIS AVENUE.

NOT ALL THE BUILDINGS IN DORMER HARRIS AVENUE ARE ALIKE.

This road is extremely close to the house at Nether Fletchhamstead which was the home of the Harris family so emotively described in her article on "Westwood and Tile Hill."

LEAMINGTON SPA

At the present time, Number 16 Gaveston Road is once again the venue for lively games of charades, parties and play-readings. Patsy Spiller, the present owner is a vivacious and experienced teacher of English and recently she said she had written a play for her students "The Case of the Crackpot Diamonds," surely a title which would have given MDH great amusement? Previously Patsy Spiller had written numerous articles for local newsapers and today her piano stands in more or less the same position as the Collard and Collard in its *"gold-brown walnut case,"* once stood on which Mary Dormer Harris and her mother once used to play sweet Victorian melodies.

A PLAQUE ON THE HOUSE?

Recently, Mrs Spiller explained to me that she had become very interested in Mary Dormer Harris and thought it entirely appropriate that a plaque denoting her residence be affixed to the exterior of the house. We both vowed to do all we could to bring this plan to fruition in 2002 and we hoped that the Leamington Literary Society and the Leamington Society would both take up the cause.

10. A MODERN POST SCRIPT

THE INFLUENCE OF MARY DORMER HARRIS IS STILL BEING FELT

"She pointed me in the right direction.

She was one of the first of the modern historians.

She was not afraid to speculate and make comments."

So said prominent Coventry writer and historian, David McGrory, of Mary Dormer Harris.

David and I were chatting in St Mary's Hall, Coventry in early May 2001 and he was telling me of his ideas that the Guild Chair, or Chair of State, had almost certainly orginated in the Coventry Priory. In her books on Coventry MDH had taken the official line that the magnificently carved chair had been used by the Guild master but she had also speculated that perhaps it might have come from the Priory. This had pointed him in the right direction and over a period of time, careful observation and much investigation had resulted in his being convinced that the chair had connections with the Bishops of Lichfield.

David McGrory and I then turned our attention to the huge tapestry in the Great Hall and once again I was delighted when he said that in his opinion MDH had been right when she had indentified the central figure of the king with Henry VI and not Henry VII as some historians of the twentieth century had claimed.

In her first book on Coventry, published in 1898, MDH had written *"The hypothesis that the pair may be intended for the then reigning Henry VII and his queen, Elizabeth of York is untenable, as the heraldic roses in the border are Lancastrian and not Tudor."*

Having helped in the compilation of dictionaries and having studied mediaeval manuscripts for nearly ten years, she was perhaps in a better position than most to judge and state her opinion clearly.

David explained that he had made some interesting discoveries about the indentity of the other figures depicted on the tapestry and once again I listened, quite captivated by his arguments, pleased that he considered MDH had come to the right conclusions and glad that he was in the process of writing another of his books on the history of the city.

In the weeks and months that followed, I visited St Mary's Hall on many occasions and I came to realise that in that ancient building I always felt close to the spirit of Mary Dormer Harris. That same large and atmospheric hall had been the scene of so many of her triumphs, and I often tried to picture her diminutive figure on the platform; her attractive voice enthusiastically describing Coventry history and thereby entertaining and informing so many.

In the mullioned-windowed Treasury, it is easy to picture her as a young woman in 1890, as she laboured over mediaeval documents for many hours on end, with her long black skirt brushing against the beautiful tiled-floor. Had she known then how posterity was to view her life's work, I think that she would have been content. Every writer likes to think they have left behind books which will ensure them posthumous fame, but unlike her, few achieve this feat. Today some of her books, in particular the Coventry Leet Book, fetch three figure sums, and all are very saleable on the second-hand book market.

Yet she was so much more than a writer and lecturer and I try never to lose sight of the intelligent, kind and energetic woman, with the loud laugh which was so infectious that people sometimes turned round in a bus to see who was making all the noise. When she died, it was small wonder that many of those who had known her, missed her lively and caring personality so much that they did all they could to keep her memory alive.

She seemed to make such a great impression on all those who knew her, so perhaps our last glimpse of Mary Dormer Harris should be as the reliable friend, beloved by so many young students, whom Gertude Bark described in 1987 as being,

...characteristically learned, generous-hearted, compassionate, and superbly humorous - or should one say, delighting in mischief and whole-hearted fun?

THE MAGNIFICENTLY-CARVED STATE CHAIR IN ST MARY'S HALL, AS DRAWN BY ALBERT CHANLER IN 1911.

11. THE WARWICKSHIRE OF MARY DORMER HARRIS

A SERIES OF EXTRACTS FROM "Some Manors, Churches and Villages of Warwickshire With an Account of Certain Old Buildings of Coventry"

INTRODUCTION

Shortly before her untimely death in 1936, Mary Dormer Harris was elected to the Council of the re-established Coventry City Guild. In 1937, as a tribute to her memory, the City Guild published a book which included five personal tributes to her, a few illustrations and the text of sixty-six articles describing a variety of places within Warwickshire. All the articles had been first published in the "Coventry Herald" between July 1930 and March 1936. Despite the fact that the book sold for twelve shillings and sixpence, quite a large amount to many in the economic depression of the 1930s, almost all of the five hundred copies of the book were sold within a few months. They have remained collectors' items ever since.

Many consider that these historical articles were some of the most interesting pieces which MDH ever wrote. Written within the last six years of her life, when she was well past her sixtieth birthday, they also contained human interest stories, philosophical remarks and a variety of references to famous writers; all written with great literary skill.

As all her works have long been out of print, with copies obtainable only on the second-hand book market, short extracts from this posthumous volume are included here so that many more readers can appreciate the fine quality of her writing, Most of the comments which she made in these articles are as valid today as the day she wrote them, but where places have changed, no attempt has been made to tamper with the text. Thus her words present a vivid picture of Warwickshire in the 1930s and now, over sixty-five years later, they have developed an added historical significance.

The extracts reproduced here appear in the order in which they appear in the book, with the exception of the longer section concerning "Westwood and Tile Hill" which is placed last for reasons which will be become obvious.

ARBURY HALL

Even on days when the sunlight colours the tree-trunks and paints on the grass the shadowed outlines of myriad beeches, there is little to enjoy in the tract of country between Coventry and Nuneaton that is filled with reminiscences of George Eliot. The town stretches on, bedraggled, indeterminate, alternating with depressing little patches of green. Still the landmarks are left. Chilvers Coton, or Shepperton Church, which Mary Ann Evans attended as a child; the churchyard where they still point out the grave of the young wife, who was the original of Milly in "Amos Barton": and Griff House, the early home of the novelist remain.

Then in Arbury Park you are in a world of green, and close to the Hall lie pleasant lawns and the beautiful stretches of water described in "Mr Gilfil's Love Story". One of these pools has been there since the days when a brotherhood of Augustinian canons flourished at Arbury, though the religious house, founded by Ralph de Sudeley in the time of Henry II has entirely disappeared...

...A HOUSE FULL OF TREASURES - The chapel at Arbury is markedly classic of the later seventeenth century with decorations of carved cherub heads, fruit and flowers. Some of the work is by Grinling Gibbons. The brass door-lock is a treasure, a specimen of the art of John Wilkes of Birmingham. Another example of his workmanship, very ingenious, but not so decorative as the one at Arbury, is in the Art Gallery of his native city. The house at Arbury is full of other treasures: Jacobite wine-glasses from Ansley Hall, the quaint old picture - engraved in Dugdale's "Warwickshire" - of the combats waged in Smithfield against other knights by Sir John de Astley in 1438 and 1441, and a portrait of the Lady Skeffington whose memorial tablet in St Michael's has such a quaint and pretty allusion to the "true moaneing turtle" who had been her husband. Very famous are the old table and chair, placed near the entrance to the long gallery, used by the Duke of Suffolk, father of Lady Jane Grey, when he hid in a hollow oak hard by Astley Church, after his failure to raise the Midlands against Queen Mary...

...Such is the dwelling at Arbury, a work of many periods, where associations seem to gather like moss on old stones, and which, because of the childish memories of a great genius, has become, as it were, part and parcel of the literary tradition of England.

ASTON HALL

...CHRISTMAS EVE AT ASTON - There are some grisly stories about Aston, into which, since you are apparently not shown the parts of the house to which they refer, we need not now enter. Let us close this little history on the more cheerful note of Christmas Eve festivity in the Holtes' time, recorded in "Popular Antiquities" by Brand. After supper a table was set in the hall, and on it a brown loaf placed with twenty threepenny pieces stuck on the top. Two of the oldest servants sat behind the loaf acting as judges. Then the steward brought in the men and maid-servants one by one; each of them had face and figure entirely hidden by a winnow sheet, save for the right hand, which was exposed and laid on the loaf. If the judges failed to guess the name of the person to whom the hand belonged, he or she was entitled to one of the threepenny bits; if they recognised the hand the discomfited claimant retired without reward. When all the money was gone the servants had liberty to drink, dance, sing and go to bed when they pleased.

BADDESLEY CLINTON HALL

Baddesley Clinton Hall, the dwelling of Captain Edward Ferrers, still lies in secluded country typically Warwickshire, and at its best in the months of May and June, though the encroaching city comes ever nearer. Coming from Warwick, you take the turn to the left by the "Tom o' Bedlam" at Chadwick End, on the Birmingham Road. The inn is modernised, but the name, if you know your Shakespeare, should recall Edgar's "poor Tom's a-cold" in "King Lear." The lane leads to the drive through the chestnut-dotted park of the manor-house, the lodge-gates being oddly constructed of two wheels taken from the carriage belonging to Mrs Rebecca Dulcibella Dering, the late owner of the place.

This well known survivor of a Victorian past, once the good fairy of Baddesley, set her face against the fast-moving traffic of these latter days. She did not willingly suffer motors to approach her ancient dwelling, and only once was she known to step into a taxicab, on the occasion of a visit to the House of Lords, to offer testimony in the Ferrers peerage case.

BADDESLEY CLINTON HALL AS PHOTOGRAPHED BY PHILIP CHATWIN, PROBABLY IN THE 1930s

BILLESLEY MANOR

...When places have queer names and folk-tales attached to them, you can generally find tales of vanished men.

Billesley ... has a tumulus, which looks extremely intriguing when you behold it, tree-grown, above the wall at the corner of the garden of the manor house. Unfortunately, like many objects apparently of high antiquity, it is a fraud, though not necessarily an intentional one. It is not built of earth, but of shale from a neighbouring pond, and careful recent excavations revealed the hoof and shoe of a horse. The latter pronounced by a British Museum authority to be of seventeenth or eighteenth century make, places it beyond a doubt that here we have the burial place of a favourite horse, piously and affectionately interred by a former owner of Billesley Manor, to the confusion of future generations. How life and hard fact scatter our fairest dreams!

CLOPTON HOUSE

...THE ANCIENT ATTICS - The second attic has an evil reputation. Ineffaceable traces of blood staining the boards between the stairhead and the door of this room, show where, according to tradition, a priest was done to death. William Clopton held fast by the Catholic faith in Elizabeth's time, and paid fines as a recusant for not attending the services of the Established Church, so that a priest may well have lived in one of the upper chambers of the house. It is almost unnecessary to add that the room is haunted.

Another visitant from the Beyond is (or was, for most likely her haunted chamber was destroyed by Mr Warde) the spirit of Charlotte Clopton, buried, so the story runs, in a trance mistaken for death. As a similar tale is told at St Giles' Cripplegate, London, where a descendant of the neighbouring family of Lucy is buried, one is inclined to believe that the incident of Juliet's awaking in the tomb must have laid hold of the local imagination. Another daughter of the house, who drowned herself for love in an unromantic-looking well in the garden, says the tale, is always likened to Ophelia, another Shakespearean heroine. Her name was Margaret. That a Margaret Clopton existed is beyond a doubt. You may see her effigy in miniature above those of her father and mother in the church at Stratford, but the veracious historian is compelled to admit that the Christian name, Charlotte, which was common in Hanoverian times, but not earlier, does not occur in the known pedigree of the family.

The latter's tragic history, however, made a deep and lasting impression on a schoolgirl of genius who visited the house with her companions somewhere about 1825, when a bevy of young gentlewomen wandered about dim corridors and twilight chambers, thrilled with their eeriness. This visitor was Elizabeth Cleghorn Stevenson, better known as Mrs Gaskell, authoress of "Cranford", whose letter describing her experiences was published by William Howitt. Elizabeth, at that time a pupil of the Misses Byerley, great nieces of Wedgwood, the potter, went to school in the now demolished house close to Stratford Church, whereof the site is now occupied by Avon Bank...

CHARLECOTE PARK

It is pleasant to leave town behind you when the young leaves of the oaks are golden-brown, and nowhere is the wooded Warwickshire country more beautiful than in the lanes by Charlecote...

...The line springs into fame with Sir Thomas Lucy, who came into his inheritance in 1551...

...A SHAKESPEARE TRADITION - Sir Thomas's fame rests... on the tradition - whether mythical or containing a kernel of truth, who will say? - that he punished Shakespeare for a poaching affray on his deer. The story first comes to us from Davies, the Vicar of Sapperton in Gloucestershire in 1696, and is evidently derived from talk current in Stratford at the end of the seventeenth century. Davies says that Shakespeare was "much given to all unluckiness in stealing venison and rabbits, particularly from Sir - Lucy, who had him often whipped and imprisoned and at last made him fly his native country to his great advancement..."

...The deer-stealing story is not impossible, though we must disregard later embroideries. Shakespeare must have had abounding joy of life, a quality which in the young is not incompatible with a disregard for the sacred rights of property, as all acquainted with details of a University "rag" will know.

CHARLECOTE GATEHOUSE AS DEPICTED ON A POSTCARD DATED 1908.

THE HOUSE AND GATEHOUSE - Sir Henry Fairfax Lucy tells me the Gatehouse at Charlecote was designed by John of Padua, an architect who came to this country under Henry VIII, and of whom practically nothing is known. This building, deservedly famous, has a central round-arched entrance and flanking turrets, with domical roofs topped by weather vanes. The main roof is edged with perforated cresting, and the whole is built of brick with stone dressings, the bricks set in alternate rows of long "stretchers" and short "heads." Everywhere in the old part of Charlecote, the variety and colour of the brickwork is delightful...

...It would be ungrateful of me to pass over the modern bust of Mary Somerville, born a Fairfax, who died in 1872, and after whom Somerville College for women at Oxford is named. She studied determinedly in days when learning in girls was frowned on, read Newton's works in Latin, and won fame by her writings on science. Those of us who live in easier days should remember the hard digging of the pioneers.

COOMBE ABBEY

Coombe Abbey lies still in its splendid park - may it long so continue - though the country round has the miscellaneous character brought by the encroaching town. West of the house is an immense sheet of water covering ninety acres. It is spanned at one end by a balustrade with classic urns atop, a marvellously picturesque touch. The sloping banks of the moat, into which the lake water has been diverted, are covered with crocuses, berberis and purple winter-heath, and the box-edges of the flower-beds of the formal garden take on the fantastic shapes of the shamrock, the thistle and the rose. A flight of steps adds a further formal grace...

...INTERIOR OF THE HOUSE - The interior of the house bears traces of considerable alteration...Very charming is the white-panelled hunting-parlour, where the panes of the windows have been delicately engraved with Craven heraldry, sporting scenes, a splendid hare and a variety of dogs...The artist was undoubtedly Chamberlain of Kenilworth who died some fifty years ago.

...Chamberlain's apprentice and successor, Mr Paul Hagg, who married his master's widow, is still living, though too much of an invalid to give any information about his art. A specimen of his work was given as a wedding present from the Brethren of Leycester Hospital, Warwick to the Princess Royal in 1922, and there are some fortunate local owners of his art. It is a matter of regret that neither at the Ceramic Department of the South Kensington Museum nor at Birmingham Art Gallery is there any knowledge of the work of these craftsmen....

...Perhaps the most charming place of all is the north- parlour, bare of furniture, all white and gold, with delicate brass door-plates, and over the mantelpiece a display of heraldry. It is like a little bit of Versailles transplanted into alien ground.....

COMPTON VERNEY FROM A POST-CARD DATED 1910.

COMPTON VERNEY

All months have their special quality of charm, but surely October, when stillness reigns after storm, the sky is deep blue, the chestnuts glowing red, and the stubble bright in the fields, is one of the pleasantest of the whole year. Hardly can there be in Warwickshire more delightful October country than that about Compton Verney, or any great house, so redolent as that is of the aristocratic case, leisure, security and cultivated taste, so marked a feature of English eighteenth century life....

...Compton Verney, or Compton Murdac as it was originally called, from the name of its earliest lords, was once held by Alice Perrers, mistress of the senile King Edward III, who is said to have stolen the ring from the finger of her lord as he lay dying. In Henry VI's reign it passed to the Verneys who held until a few years ago. Through a marriage of Sir Richard Verney, who died in 1630, with Margaret Greville, sister of Sir Fulke Greville, of Warwick Castle and a descendant of the Willoughby de Broke family, that peerage was revived in the person of their grandson, Sir Richard Verney, who died in 1711. Of this Sir Richard, "happily qualified with the most ingenious inclination," Dugdale speaks with cordiality, and it must be owning to Verney's liberal treatment of him that so many illustrations relating to the house and family appear in "The Antiquities of Warwickshire." The author of that magnificent work, be it noted, not only recognised the generosity of those who aided its publication, but did not hesitate to stigmatise the "frugality" of any member of an ancient house who refused to pay for the cost of the plates to illustrate the home or burial- place of his ancestors. How pleasant it must be to have one's forebears praised, and how dreadful to have them thus pilloried, in the immortal volume...

....THE TWO HOUSES - The arrangement of the gardens, with the spreading lawns, to which the favourite epithet of "verdant" so well applies, and the damming of the stream to form a sheet of ornamental water, was carried out by Lancelot (called 'Capability') Brown, who died in 1783. Brown who rose from humble beginnings to a position of great authority in his art, may well be regarded as the chief founder of the English style of landscape gardening. He always stressed the existing features of the landscape, and his success at Compton, where kindly nature lent him such aid, has made the setting of the house more delightful than any other example of the period I can recall...

AN ADAM PORTICO - To approach the house, you cross the beautiful sheet of water by a stone bridge, no doubt designed by Adam and decorated with leaden figures of sphinxes. The main entrance with the Corinthian colonnade, the most pleasing part of the house, and the projecting wings, north and south, are the work of the same architect. The delicate workmanship of the Adam portico, the carefully thought out effects such as the tapering of the row of columns before the entrance door, are a joy to lovers of the classic style.....Among eighteenth century interiors, this house has few rivals in England...

COUGHTON COURT

...FEATURES OF THE HOUSE - Built at a time when concealment was of the first necessity, the house is full of traces of priests' holes. The turret at the north-east corner of the Tower Chamber is hollow from top to bottom, and when opened some seventy years since, revealed two ladders tied together, three altar stones, a folding Spanish leather altar and a palliasse bed whereon some hunted priest must have lain long ago. Father Garnet was at the Court in November 1605, when the house was lent to Sir Everard Digby, and tradition says that the ladies, whose sympathies lay with the Gunpowder plotters, waited in what is now the drawing room till Bates, Catesby's servant, came in a gallop to tell them all was lost, and rode off to rejoin his master.

LINKS WITH THE OLD RELIGION - Within the maze of rooms are numberless treasures, some recalling the suffering of old days...In a window at the foot of the staircase may be seen the heraldry of the families of Catesby and Tresham, with others allied to the Throckmortons, blazoned in coloured glass. The staircase from Harvington Hall, a Worcestershire Catholic stronghold, now in a room at Coughton, also calls up memories of those troubled days.

Relics of the continuity of the religious life at Coughton are to be found all over this wonderful treasure-house... In the dining room stands a chair made from the oak of Richard III's bed. I suppose the wood came from the "White Boar," Leicester, where he slept before riding out to Bosworth. In the Tribune, hangs a chemise of

Mary, Queen of Scots. Always romance attached to the unhappy, and those who died violent deaths...

A FAMOUS COAT - One must also tell of a famous coat which hangs in the Hall. It was made for a wager laid by Sir John Throckmorton in 1811. At sunrise it was wool on a sheep's back; by sunset it was a smart blue cut-away coat worn by the triumphant winner of the wager...

COVENTRY, PALACE YARD

Seeing the rather shabby modernised Earl Street front of Palace Yard, you would never guess what a wonderful house it is. Even if you enter the gabled quadrangle, and your eye is caught by the beautiful lead gutters and spouting - not forgetting that charming little strip of ventilator in a window in the middle of the west side - you will not have exhausted the interest of the place. You must go through the second archway - it is a pity that the glass roof beyond prevents your seeing the little strip of vine-patterned lead-work above - and go up the stairs to the ante-room with the classic fireplace and King James's Room with the beautiful ceiling, to get some idea of what a wealthy citizen's house was like in the second half of the seventeenth century.

And that is not all. Palace Yard has to be seen by sections. You must go back into Earl Street and beg the people in the bookshop - the many times I have encroached upon their kindness! - to let you see the mediaeval stone chimney-pieces in the north-west corner of the house, which was once, I believe, a separate

A RARE PHOTOGRAPH OF PALACE YARD, COVENTRY AROUND 1913.

dwelling. Everywhere tie-beams, posts, and flooring show the strength and solidity of the old oak. It is regrettable that the panelling has been stripped from the walls of King James's room, and that the staircase with the floreated filling, taking the place of balusters, illustrated in the "Troughton Drawings," should have been sold off for a new house away from the neighbourhood. The "Palace lawn," mentioned in 1822, has also been built over. Yet despoiled and encroached on as it is, the beauty that is left and its memories, cause Palace Yard to rank high among the historic houses of Warwickshire.

NEARLY DEMOLISHED! - And yet it was nearly lost. In 1915 we feared it would be demolished, as decayed and useless, to make way for the speculative builder. Strings were pulled, however; patriotic and generous people came forward, including the late Bishop Yeatman-Biggs. The house was preserved and repaired and part of it is now a centre for the work of the Coventry diocese. Otherwise, Palace Yard would have gone the way of the old Cathedral, Whitefriar's Church and beautiful Coventry houses without number...

ETTINGTON PARK

...A UNIQUE LENGTH OF TENURE - In one respect, Ettington is unique. Saswalo held Lower Ettington in 1086, when the Domesday Survey was taken, and his descendants hold it still. I believe that no other land-owning family in England can boast of a descent in the male line from a Domesday holder...

....Another signal honour belongs to the Shirleys. An ancestor of theirs is mentioned by Shakespeare (1 Hen. iv, Act 5 sc 4) in one of the scenes telling of the Battle of Shrewsbury....

...THE HOUSE - The house is by no means as old as the family who possess it. It has been Gothicised, and a casual visitor sees little of it that does not belong to the eighteenth or nineteenth century...

....Ettington when you read of it and see it, seems to give the history of England in a nutshell, so the Shirleys have fought and adventured at home and abroad, but it is the sight of the ruined church in the garden that stirs the imagination.

THE RUINED CHURCH - The building is ivy-smothered, and a few arches of the roofless nave arcade stand out in a world of green. The tower is open on its eastern side; the south transept however, where the family tombs lie, is still intact, and is fitted up as a chapel...

THE UNDERHILLS - The tower now serves as a kind of mausoleum for the Underhills, who had a lease of this place in the sixteenth and seventeenth centuries, and were, in their way, as remarkable a family as the Shirleys, and also, it seems, passionately addicted to genealogy. One of a Kenilworth branch of the family emigrated to America in 1630, served as a military instructor in New England and fought against the Pequot Indians. There is an Underhill Society in America and a large volume has been written about their history, which I have not studied as I should have done...

.....In an embrasure of a window is a little urn placed in memory of William Croft, the musician, born at Lower Ettington in 1678. The tunes he composed, "St Anne," "Hanover," and "Eatington," sung to "O God, our Help," "O Worship the King," and "Let Saints on earth," will be familiar to all. Thus Ettington, which embraces so much of the history, calls also to mind the arts of England.

KNOWLE, GRIMSHAW HALL

"My grey has got ye Day." These words scratched with a diamond, appear on a pane of glass in a window of the beautiful old house, Grimshaw Hall, which you pass as you leave Knowle by the Hampton Road. The victorious grey I suppose was a horse belonging to either Nancy or Fanny Grimshaw, whose names, written with fine eighteenth-century flourishes, may be read above on the same pane....

...The "grey" was in all likelihood a racehorse of that colour, though it is possible that the exigencies of rhyme may have caused the docking by one syllable of the word "greyhound." Coursing the hare with hounds was a far older and better established sport in England than horse-racing; Shakespeare knew everything there is to be known about the former pastime and spends much pity on the hunted hare, whereas he only once alludes to "riding wagers" where horses are nimbler than the running sands of the hour-glass or clock. It was James 1 who made horse-racing popular in England, as it had long been in his own country over the Border. Coleshill was, apparently, a centre for races in Queen Anne's time; at least Addison, in the

GRIMSHAW HALL, KNOWLE

"Spectator" in 1711 alludes to a plate offered there as a prize for the fleetest horse. Coleshill is not far from Grimshaw Hall; possibly it was there Miss Nancy's grey carried off the victory. Well, well, they are dead - these girls with their light hearts and their laughter, dead, along with the Whigs and the Tories, Marlborough, Mr Addison of the "Spectator" and the great Queen Anne herself. Thinking of them, "I feel chilly and grown old," as Browning says, speaking of the dear dead women of old Venice, who had such golden hair.

A GHOST STORY - There is a ghost story connected with Grimshaw Hall - there would be! A beautiful lady, dressed for a ball, "walks" in one of the bedrooms. They say she was murdered by a jealous lover, who afterwards fought with his rival in the stable yard, which has likewise a reputation for uncanny visitants...

LONG ITCHINGTON, WHITE HALL AND THE GABLED TUDOR HOUSE

It was on the twenty-first of December, St Thomas's Day, which is the time when village people went "a - Thomasing," in ancient days to beg for corn or good things for Christmas, and when bread-doles are still distributed in many places, that I went to Long Itchington. The country-side had put on an array of winter beauty, the bare branches of the trees, clothed in rime, made lacelike patterns amongst the mist, and the village itself, with its ancient black and white timbered houses and the boys sliding on the pool, made up a typical picture of wintry rural England.

ST WULFSTAN - What other connections, save the bread dole, Long Itchington has with St Thomas, who preached Christianity to the Ethiopians and was martyred in India, I know not, but the village has a saint of its own, one Wulfstan, born about 1008 and canonised 1203, the only Warwickshire man - as far as I know - who ever received canonisation from the Pope....

...LARGER POPULATION THAN COVENTRY In the eleventh century, when the Domesday Survey was made, Long Itchington boasted of a much larger population than Godiva's Coventry...

MAXSTOKE CASTLE

Something has gone from the country life in England. The chain of continuity, observable even so recently as the period before the Great War, has been snapped. The nineteenth century saw considerable changes; the gradual emptying of the villages; the collapse in the seventies and eighties of many who had been formerly prosperous of the tenant-farming stock; but still there was an appearance of permanence, even though in some cases it may have been deceptive. But now we can no longer close our eyes to a further change that is coming over England. The families whose names are historic, are leaving the land; others come in to their inheritance. The last relics of feudal England are passing away.

It is a mighty change. In the Middle Ages, when the ancestors or forerunners of those families held vast estates, the lives and well being of hundreds might depend on a military lord's nod. In Stuart times, the squire, as Justice of the Peace, sitting

MAXSTOKE PRIORY AS PHOTOGRAPHED BY PHILIP CHATWIN, PROBABLY IN 1930. The figure on the left is almost certainly Mary Dormer Harris who sometimes accompanied Philip Chatwin on architectural or archaeological excursions. The other woman may be Mrs Chatwin.

in his wainscoted parlour, with his pipe and tankard of ale, ruled over the neighbourhood like a little king. Even in Victoria's days which some of us can remember, and others read of in such books as Anthony Trollope's Barsetshire Novels, or Richard Jeffries' "Hodge and His Masters," how stable, how authoritative, seemed the position and power of a landowner bearing an ancient name. Well, times are different. There is no more to say.

THE DILKE FAMILY - Happily, the Dilkes - or Fetherston-Dilkes, for the first name was added with an inheritance from the Fetherstons of Packwood - still hold Maxstoke Castle...

...Maxstoke was begun by William de Clinton, of the family who have left their name in Baddesley Clinton, who built Caesar's Tower at Kenilworth Castle, the priories of Kenilworth and Maxstoke, and whose effigies - one of remarkable beauty - lie in Coleshill Church...

STONELEIGH ABBEY

At Stoneleigh Abbey the fanciful might be haunted by the vision of a slight womanly figure in a short-waisted dress. Perhaps as she is already thirty, she will

STONELEIGH ABBEY, FROM A POSTCARD DATED 1905.

wear a cap. Her cheeks are round and full, her eyes shine, and her laugh - ye gods! - to live in a house that has sheltered Jane Austen...

QUEEN VICTORIA'S VISIT - Another famous figure haunts some of the large and lofty rooms. The Queen. Other queens have reigned, but this is the Queen par excellence, the little plump, majestic woman, who could make great cheering crowds fall silent by the dignity of her presence. They show you in the Abbey, the bedroom Victoria slept in; a period room, very interesting; all white and gold save the great four-poster bed. In the corridor is the breakfast-service she used, and in the Saloon are the costly white, hand-embroidered chairs the late Lord Leigh had made for her coming. There will be few now living who can remember the visit of 1858, so long the talk of the countryside. I believe the Yeomanry formed a guard of honour, and during the visit there was a terrific thunderstorm. In the evening the Queen showed herself on the balcony to the cheering crowd.

STRATFORD-ON-AVON, SHAKESPEARE'S HOUSE AND ANNE HATHAWAY'S COTTAGE

It is pleasant to go to Stratford in the blackthorn winter, when winds are high, for hedges are white with blossom and the sunlight brings out in the grass an intenser green. Later, sightseers come: but even they do not quite destroy the charm of the place. At the Birthday there is a pell-mell of people there - all sorts, just as

THE PROCESSION TO SHAKESPEARE'S TOMB APRIL 23RD 1907.

ANNE HATHAWAY'S COTTAGE FROM A POST CARD DATED AUGUST 1915.

there are in Shakespeare's plays. And they behave, not as English people usually do, with self-conscious reserve, but become enthusiastic, even a trifle sentimental. Flags fly, speeches are made, and processions of men, women and children start off, carrying flowers to the grave in the church. Well, well, why not? After all, Shakespeare is our race's chiefest glory; his words have gone forth to the end of the world. Why should we not put aside our habitual dread of showing our feelings, and just be proud and glad?...

Then the house is left in Henley Street - the neat, tight, unremarkable Tudor house, built for middling-folk to dwell in, that is now the supreme treasure of all the historic houses in England. What luck that it should be left to us, when so much that was magnificent and commanding has been done away with!...

...ANNE HATHAWAY'S COTTAGE - The crown-imperials made a brave show, too, in Anne Hathaway's Cottage garden, and in a remoter corner among the grass were daffodils and celandines....The thatch-roofed, timbered farmhouse, built on foundations of stone is of extraordinary interest...

...The house was purchased in 1892 by the Shakespeare Trustees, for which we may be for ever grateful.

WARWICK CASTLE

It seems almost impertinent to praise Warwick Castle, as has been done so admirably by Dugdale, who said Fulke Greville made it "the most princely seat within the Midlands parts of the realm," and by Sir Walter Scott. Two portions of it linger most in the mind, to my thinking, after a visit. The first is the Mill Street view of Caesar's Tower, high and splendid , rock -founded, lording it over over the ravine and river. It seems ungracious to record to what cruel uses the building was once put, and how prisoners have languished in its dungeons. Can grisly memories adhere to beauty like this?

There is nothing sinister, however, about the Italian garden, of which the beauty bursts on anyone entering on the grounds from the greenhouse side. From the terrace there is a view of the distant woods. If you happen to spy a peacock among the green, that gives a supreme touch...

HISTORY - The Earls of Warwick have made history. Some of them were powerful men, often too powerful for the comfort of unstable kings. Piers Gaveston, favourite of Edward II, called one of them "The Black Dog of Arden" but the mocker lost his head. Thomas Beauchamp, builder of Guy's Tower - his memorial brass is in St Mary's Church - sought to curb Richard II, but the king triumphed for the moment, and sent Earl Thomas to the Tower of London, and the Beauchamp Tower, where he was imprisoned, is still called after his name. Richard Beauchamp, who has the most gorgeous tomb in England, has been recalled to men's mind of late by Bernard Shaw's "St Joan." The King-maker, Richard Neville, "last of the barons," as we all know, made and unmade kings. The Duke of Clarence, "false, fleeting, perjured," held the castle once for a time in right of his wife, Isabel Neville,

THE VIEW OF CAESAR'S TOWER, WARWICK CASTLE, FROM MILL STREET, IN THE EARLY YEARS OF THE TWENTIETH CENTURY.

until his brother, Edward IV, saw fit to cut short his life. So did Anne, wife of Richard III, surely the most unhappy of all the heiresses of the Warwick line. She was still a child at the death of her first husband, the Lancastrian Prince of Wales, at the battle of Tewksbury. Her brother in law, Clarence, hid her in London, disguised, lest his brother Richard should marry her and dispute with him the Warwick inheritance.

But Richard tracked her and - one cannot but think against her will - married her. The pair stayed at Warwick during the summer of the murder of Richard's nephews, the little Princes in the Tower. Anne's only child died the following year. She did not long survive him. Clarence's son, also Earl of Warwick, was only a lad, whom Henry VII, fearing he might be a pretender to the Crown, trumped up a charge against him and put him to death. The Dudleys came in under Edward VI and the Grevilles, Lords Brooke, under James I. One of the latter line, honourably mentioned by Milton, was killed at the Siege of Lichfield in 1643, fighting on the side of Parliament. Thereafter, times have been more peaceful for the possessors of Warwick.

THE NORMAN DOORWAY OF ST MARY'S CHURCH STONELEIGH, WITH THE "WONDROUS WRITHING SERPENTS" IN THE TYMPANUM.

ST MARY'S, STONELEIGH

Stoneleigh is one of the most beautifully situated of all Warwickshire churches...

...The best piece of exterior architecture is the Norman north door, of which the tympanum, which fills the space beneath the curve of the arch, is carved with wondrous writhing serpents, and monsters such as, in actuality, the eye can never behold. There is a little twisted serpent all alone on the top. Is there here some symbolism of the expulsion of evil? The north of the church is considered the less honourable side, and more subject to the influences of evil spirits.

WARMINGTON

It is claimed for Warmington, which lies at the foot of a spur of Edge Hill, just off the line of the Warwick and Banbury road, that it is the most beautiful village in Warwickshire and certainly the claim is not without justification. The village is stone-built and of the Cotswold type. A wonderful sixteenth-century manor-house overlooks the broad central green, with its pool for sheep-washing. The comfortable-looking vicarage and the ancient cottages grouped round the green all go to make up a picture of rare pleasantness, remarkable even in a county where there is still a wealth of varied village beauty left.

...From the village a pathway and flight of thirty-seven steps leads up to the churchyard on the brow of the hill. From this height you may see between the trees glimpses of the rolling wood-grown Warwickshire country stretching at your feet for miles and miles. In the churchyard this steep path is bordered with catmint, the blue-grey of the flowers making a lovely contrast to the dark-hued, leaning stones that mark ancient graves. One of these is a memorial of a famous fight of long ago - the battle of Edge Hill - and on the south side a strip of close-mown grass leads to a worn tomb-stone whereon are engraved the words: "Here lieth the body of Alexander Gourdin, Capitaine, buried the 25th day of October, Anno Domi 1642." ... It is not known how many died on that autumn Sunday 290 years ago. Probably only a few hundred on each side perished. An old author says, however, he had "heard that the country people thereabouts, by burying of the naked bodies, found the number to be about six thousand that fell on both sides, besides those that died afterwards of their wounds." The dead would be buried where they lay; it must have been the wounded, who struggled or were borne away, who lie in the village churchyards near. The register of Newbold Pacey has an entry in 1642: "A souldier wounded in that great battell between the King and the parliament, Oct. 23, was buried Oct. 29." There must have been many hasty burials of nameless men in those unquiet days...

ST MARY'S WARWICK

...GUARDING THE CHURCH'S TREASURES - High in the wall west of the sepulchre are gratings through which the sacristan could keep watch over the church's treasures, and on the south side are three openings into a private mediaeval pew and a squint near by for a sight of the high altar at the east end. In the centre of the choir is the alabaster tomb of the founder, Thomas Beauchamp (died 1369). The effigy shows the earl as if clad in plate armour with jupon (or coat) bearing his arms. His ungauntleted hand clasps that of his wife, Catherine (Mortimer); an unmuzzled bear lies at his feet.

ASHOW

Ashow lies in a pocket off the main road from Warwick, by Finham to Coventry. Southwards, among yellow sedges past a little island, near where a fallen tree lies across the stream. The current is swift here, for stones make a miniature waterfall, with its gentle music. Beyond the churchyard, with the old cross and great yew tree at the south corner, a wooden bridge spans the water, and a pathway leads over fields to the Leamington road. The Avon hereabouts takes its toll of life, as all deep waters do, and for many years there was kept at the Dial House, a "dead cart" with tall sides hiding from view the body of any drowned man on the journey from the place of death. In the calamitous year of 1879 all the river rose in terrific flood, and the hay stood uncarried on wagons for nearly six weeks in the impassable meadows. Some hot-headed gentleman laid a wager he would drive his tandem over Chesford Bridge. Mid-way through the flood the trouble came. Though the shafts helped to steady the wheeler, the second horse, the coachman had to descend at great peril to cut the leader free, and the beautiful creature was swept over the hedge, its drowned body floating down as far as Blackdown Mill. The foolhardy occupant of the carriage escaped with his life.

WHEN FISHING WAS GOOD - Fishing used to be good in days before the river was polluted by sewage. Pike and perch were caught, and fishermen laid wicker traps, or pudgeons, for eels. One Rector of Ashow, a lover of the rod and line (now, as Charles Lamb might say, with God) damaged his face casting his bait for a pike. The hook hit a tree, and springing back, penetrated the flesh so deeply that it had to be cut out by the surgeon's knife. Of course this happened a long while back, when clergymen were less burdened with duties than they are today.

...TYPICAL VICTORIANS - To know a village you must have been born and bred there; otherwise you can scarcely hope to get at the heart of its life. Late-comers in life may purchase a kind of freedom by settlement. Your true villager is free-born. Of the freedom of Ashow I cannot boast; I can but tell what I have heard of two farmers of the old school, long dead - Mr Norman, of Grove House, a lifelong batchelor, and my great-uncle, James Dormer, of the Dial House. Mr Norman's Christmas Eve whist parties are still remembered. The guests (all men) supped on the contents of of a barrel of oysters, mulled ale and - tell it not in Gath! - port wine. There are no such festive gatherings in these lean days. James Dormer, of the Dial House, a man of method, kept his place in such apple-pie order that - as I heard from the late Canon Beaumont - it was pointed out to Prince Albert, when he and the Queen came to Stoneleigh in 1858, as the model of what a farm should be. (On this occasion, great-uncle James put up a stand in his front garden, where he and his friends might sit in comfort and watch the road for the passing of the Queen.) When he expected visitors, the men were ordered to go round the rickyard and snip off straggling straws from the ricks with a pair of shears. I pray that his wandering spirit may never behold the litter, and alas! the bareness of many a modern rickyard in the Warwickshire countryside he knew so well.

ASTON CANTLOW

...THE CASTLE - all that is left of the Castle of the Cantelupes, the mounds and moat were easily seen.

I would have made a more exhaustive examination of these remains had not my companion spied a bull in the far corner of the field. The animal - to which no reference had been made - appeared quite unconscious of our presence, and may have been the tamest of living creatures; still the habit of archaeological exploration in the neighbourhood of a bull is one that takes some practice to acquire! I own that, from that moment, I beat an unhurried and collected retreat stilewards, the effect of the discovery being heightened by my companion's tale of the untimely death of a farmer, who had ventured near a like animal of her acquaintance reputed so gentle as to be a household pet.

CORLEY

...THE OPEN-AIR SCHOOL - Off the little road that curves by the churchyard are fields where the view south and east is wide and beautiful. And surely few beauty spots in England have been put to such admirable use as the heights of Corley, for here is the Open-Air-School for Coventry Children, the second of its kind to be founded in England - Malvern has the credit of establishing the first - since 1918 under the care of the Coventry Education Committee. Here in summer ninety and in winter sixty, of the most delicate, under-developed children from the city schools recover health and become fat and rosy, breathing the glorious air and living on wholesome food. No child is admitted suffering from actual disease; they are just youngsters who are pining away because of the haphazard way children are born and live under city conditions, and till the world gets better, fitter for the young to live in, it is meet that such beneficent schemes as the Corley Open-Air School should take shape all over the land.

I knew the school in its humbler beginnings, soon after it was started in 1915 by Mrs T.A.Cash and Miss Thornton, who gave the land and built the first shed. It was one open shelter, of the type used for consumptives, about 60ft by 12ft. The matron slept in the middle, and the kitchen was separated from the rest of the shelter by a screen made of egg-boxes, presented by the local grocer. Sometimes the rain drove in as the children slept. But what mattered it? There were ten or twelve of them, and they throve magnificently, some putting on weight at the rate of a pound in a week. Gradually other rooms were added: then the city took the affair over. There was an official opening of the grand buildings in July 1927.

PLEASURES OF THE COUNTRYSIDE - Never will the writer of these lines forget the happy weeks of spring and summer passed in some huts in the corner of this field nearest the Church Farm before the new buildings were made. There were two or three sheds for living and sleeping in, and a kitchen made out of an old caravan. One stepped out of one's bedroom on to the grass every morning, and ahead was the lovely slope and the distant view. By night, the hut-dwellers could hear the the travelling "yap-yap" of the foxes in the woods, and by day the clamour of the cuckoo and the birds, while they basked in the sun. When energy succeeded langour, we could stroll off to the woods - I believe there is a bird sanctuary there now - or, in the civilised modern way, go off in the motor to Astley, or to Hartshill, where the decayed old castle stands, and the cottage where Michael Drayton, Warwickshire poet of happy memory, was born....

...Ah! those were pleasant days! Rarely have I enjoyed the country more, or so fully realised the changeful beauty of mid-England...

...RECOLLECTIONS In the church are some modern windows of no particular merit to the family of Moggs, and since my great-grandmother, who married Thomas Garner and migrated from Corley to Wasperton somewhere about 1802, bore that uneuphonious name, I always view them with interest. I can recall as a child being taken to see Miss Susannah, who then lived in the Quadrant Coventry. You may see her name inscribed on a heavy tomb in Corley churchyard.

LAPWORTH

...After passing through Rowington, where the old church stands massive and fortress-like on the top of the hill, you turn left over a canal bridge, and are immediately in Lapworth. On the right is a house with a garden full of neatly clipped old yews. Here, until his death in extreme old age in 1844, lived John Morteboys - the name appears in the district in the fifteenth century - who earned £20 a year for keeping the village school in a small cottage by the church. He evidently placed his pen at the service of the unlettered villager, for Robert Hudson, whose "Memorials of a Warwickshire Parish" is a type of what a village history should be, tells us how, in 1896, an old woman came late at night to the door, to ask if Mr Morteboys would write a letter for her. Poor soul, her wandering wits had turned to the memories of early days, for the old schoolmaster had lain for fifty years and more beneath the sod.

...The Lapworth people lost one splendid relic from the churchyard in the early seventeenth century. This was "a fair cross builded within arches, wherein a dozen men might have stood dry in foul weather." It was pulled down by some never-to-be-sufficiently-execrated person named Askew, who used the stones to "grownsill" his house and make his chimneys withal. There are vandals in every age.

LIGHTHORNE AND CHESTERTON

...THE FOSSE - Happily now there is nothing military about the Fosse, which when all is said and done, is the most beautiful road in Warwickshire. It is a little rash to say this, because motorists and house-builders are beginning to discover its loveliness, and when motorists and house-builders come, then begins desolation. May the gods of the old Romans who first made it - Ceres, bountiful mother of the corn, and Pan, god of the shepherds - protect the Fosse. May the Telfords of our day turn aside when they approach this road of roads. Believe me it leads practically nowhither. Till you come to the Cotswolds there is no place of any importance in its neighbourhood. Leave us its shade, its rough surface, its narrowness, its ribbon of tumbled sward, its nightingale-haunted bushes, its peeps over trailing hedges into the unknown....

...LIGHTHORNE - A turn to the left brings you to Lighthorne, where thatched cottages seem to grow out of sloping banks, a summer's day joy for an artist, though when winter settles in the villagers must feel the length of the monotonous passage of hours...

CHESTERTON WINDMILL, AS PHOTOGRAPHED BY PHILIP CHATWIN, PROBABLY IN THE 1930s.

...CHESTERTON - A road through gates and fields that have a refreshing touch of wildness, leads to Chesterton, once the home of the Peytos, a tiny group of cottages with a little church lying apart on rising ground, but a place whose history might repay a lifetime of study. What is it that makes the place so mournful? What memories haunt it?... Fate went hard with Chesterton in the Great War. You may see from the memorial in the church that seven men from this tiny village never came back...

...On the summit of a neighbouring hill is the stone windmill erected in 1632, probably from the design by Inigo Jones. If you again join the Fosse, you will also see the great camp with wide ditches the Romans made. Fragments of Roman pottery may be easily picked up in a nearby field. They make you feel how old the history of England is, and how far, far, back stretch the generations of labouring men.

NEWBOLD PACEY AND LOXLEY

...CATHERINE CARTER - But my real business here in Newbold Pacey lies with a tombstone commemorating humbler folk on the south side of the churchyard. There you may read that Catherine Carter, widow of Charles Carter, who died on February 8 1848 aged 59, lies beneath it, and with her, Charles her son, who died December 20th, 1840, aged 11. The words of the inscription below strike the ear like a cry of pain. "He was the only son of his mother and she was a widow." Catherine Carter, my grandmother's sister, was a woman of many sorrows, but of such unswerving charity and sweetness that her memory still pervades the little village, as least for those who have heard from a bygone generation of her goodness to them in the days of their childhood. One of my most treasured possessions is the tortoise -shell tea-caddy that once belonged to her - alas! one lid is gone - with a big "C" on a little silver plate below the keyhole. Old family letters refer to her marriage with Mr Carter, who must have "led her to the hymeneal altar," as the phrase then went, in the 'twenties of the last century, and one of my mother's early recollections was the death of little Charles, whose feet were bled, according to the rather barbarous medical practice of the day, to decrease the fever (I suppose cerebral) from which he died. After his death the childless woman adopted my mother's brother, Thomas Dormer, a much-loved lad with a beautiful singing voice. But again

"Comes the blind fury with th' abhorred shears
And slits the thin - spun life."

It was thought the boy contracted some illness during sheep-washing in the terrifically hot summer of 1846. He was gathered to his fathers, and in her distress the sufferer from this second blow could only beat her knees over and over again, uttering the loved names in tireless rhythm, "Tom and Charles; Tom and Charles!"

...CHRISTMAS REVELS RECALLED - Winter must have been a glorious time at the farmhouse in the village. The pond might be frozen over and one could behold fish imprisoned within its icy depths. Then, too, one heard the rhythmic fall of the battens of the flails on the barn-threshing floor , where two labourers were employed the whole winter through. On Christmas Eve the choir and musicians came round with their fiddles, to sing and play and have a merry meal, for in those days the organ had not reduced all church music to a devastating uniformity. Then there was the excitement of the mummers' visit, where the village actors, clad in night-shirts, with patches of black and red, and big balloon trousers, smiting one another with a bladder attached to a stick, danced and played a drama so old that it enshrines relics of heathendom, the Christmas play of St George, with its incidents of combat, death or wounding, and recovery or resurrection. They brought a great wooden tooth for the doctor to pull out, and by these means restore the stricken combatant to health. It is all as old as the hills. I do not think any mummers play in villages now.

STONELEIGH

Whereas Ashow is just a "snuggery" by the river, which in a measure, cuts it off from the world, Stoneleigh, a place anciently of some importance, is a "thoroughfare" village lying about a knot of roads....

...ANTIQUATED VICTORIANISM - In the old days - I hardly like to mention such antiquated Victorianism - the candles were in use for service on Lenten evenings, and the chancel arch stood out against unrelieved black. On Sunday mornings, after the psalms were said, and the Litany, and the Ten Commandments, and sometimes the prayer about the "most comfortable Sacrament," which I fancy

THE INTERIOR OF ST MARY'S CHURCH, STONELEIGH.

is seldom used now, and the chants and hymns were (perhaps indifferently) sung, we listened to the vicar's well-sounding sermon of the prevailing rotund, sentimental type. We saw him seldom; he was a shy, bookish man, who had little in common with us; but once a year, at harvest thanksgiving, we went to supper at the Vicarage. On those rare occasions, when there were collections, - always I think, for some local charity or the Agricultural Benevolent; I cannot remember the words "church expenses" were ever breathed! - my father as churchwarden, handed round the plate. Mrs Farmer put her money in; so did the Simpsons of "The Grange, " and the Misses - who sat in the pew before us. You must remember the Misses - , tall flowing women who came to church in the high waggonette. They went south afterwards, learned to play tennis and became of a gentility that passes belief, and when we chanced to meet in after years, were inclined to patronise my mother and me, as simple people, who had never mastered the art of getting on in the world.

WILMCOTE

It is the right thing to approach Wilmcote, the ancient home of Shakespeare's mother, Mary Arden, by way of Snitterfield, the ancient home of Shakespeare's father...

...WILMCOTE AND MARY ARDEN In Wilmcote, which is just an "anyhow" place, with a station, a few houses and a modern church, is Mary Arden's cottage, which is not really a cottage, but a considerable farmhouse, perhaps even a small

THE REAR OF MARY ARDEN'S HOUSE AS IT WAS IN THE 1930s WHEN MARY DORMER HARRIS DESCRIBED IT SO ELOQUENTLY.

manor house, since it possesses a dovecote, and only lords of the manor were allowed to keep doves. Tell it not in Gath, but there is some doubt whether this house was really the old Arden dwelling. "The tradition of Mary Arden's cottage," says Mr Fripp, "is that it faces the site, on the opposite side of the road, of an ancient and larger building (the foundations of which are visible in a dry summer) which was perhaps Master Robert Arden's copy-hold farm" But for our purposes the house is Mary Arden's cottage, and certainly no one could desire a fairer dwelling to help us realise the beauty, simplicity, and necessity for labour, of the home surroundings of country folk in the poet's day... The house, which contains timbers as old, I believe, as the fourteenth century - the gable-ends look later than the rest - has lately been admirably restored by the Shakespeare Trust, and the uncoloured wooden structure is now happily revealed. The cottage, the brick barns, the garden, blue with delphiniums, where fluttering white pigeons will alight and eat out of your hand, make up a picture it is a joy to behold. Nowhere is any fuss, or clutter, or unmeaning ornament. The essential beauty of structure, the simple rectilinearity of post and beam, make a restful contrast to the eye-wearying, ignoble habitations men build for themselves so often in these machine-made times...

...At the back of the house - even more charming than the frontage - is the dovecote, full of pigeon-holes, and in the barn are stored all sorts of old-time implements for landwork...

COVENTRY'S ANCIENT BUILDINGS AND THEIR STORY

Coventry, which lies on the great north-west road from London, has an important history. In the Middle Ages, the city was a centre of monastic life and the arts dependent on religion. It was also a fortress, with huge walls strengthened by thirty-two towers and having twelve gates. The citizens carried on a great trade in cloth, and displayed much energy in building, and some of their work, such as St Mary's Hall, still survives. After a long and fierce struggle, the people of the city won powers of self-government, and in 1345, they purchased from the King, the power of electing their own Mayor. Such are the general features of Coventry history at the time of its early greatness, when it ranked as the fourth city of England...

THE CATHEDRAL OF ST MICHAEL and ALL ANGELS - In the centre of Coventry, best approached through picturesque Pepper Lane, stands St Michael's, formerly a church, now a Cathedral, its nine-storied steeple a land-mark over all the country round. The steeple, nearly 300 feet high, is made up of tower, octagon or lantern, and spire, with flying buttresses between the lantern and pinnacles of the tower, and panelwork, niches with figures, renewed at the restoration of 1885-90, and its windows varying in number from story to story, make up the harmonious beauty of its decoration. It is one the most famed spires in England...

"IN THE CENTRE OF COVENTRY, BEST APPROACHED THROUGH PICTURESQUE PEPPER LANE, STANDS ST MICHAEL'S, FORMERLY A CHURCH, NOW A CATHEDRAL..."
So wrote MDH in the 1930s and this photograph shows the fine view she described.

THE EXTERIOR OF ST MARY'S HALL, AS ILLUSTRATED BY ALBERT CHANLER IN THE "THE STORY OF COVENTRY" BY MARY DORMER HARRIS, IN 1911.

ST MARY'S HALL - Opposite the south porch of Coventry Cathedral is St Mary's Hall, the surface of its beautiful red and grey sandstone front partially renewed, maybe the finest English example of a city house in timber and stone. Built as a meeting place for the united Guilds of the Holy Trinity. St Mary, St John the Baptist, and St Katharine, it takes its name from the first of these to be founded (1340) St Mary's or the Merchant Guild....

...TAPESTRY AND ARMOUR - Under the north window, stretching across the entire width of the hall, hangs a piece of sixteenth century tapestry . It represents a kneeling king, traditionally Henry VI and Margaret of Anjou, and their courtiers, with a row of male and female saints above them. The upper central panel is occupied by a seated figure of Justice, an Elizabethan insertion replacing a figure repugnant to Puritans, encompassed by kneeling angels bearing the instruments of the Passion, and the lower one by the Assumption of the Virgin, the figure surrounded by kneeling apostles.

KING HENRY VI AND QUEEN MARGARET (OF ANJOU) AS DEPICTED ON THE TAPESTRY IN ST MARY'S HALL, COVENTRY. These drawings are from the Aylesford Collection which was completed in the 1820s.

COVENTRY, HOLY TRINITY CHURCH AND THE RUINS OF THE OLD CATHEDRAL - To the north west of the Cathedral of St Michael, Coventry, stands Holy Trinity, anciently the parish church of the Priory Estate in Coventry, it cruciform character obscured by the growth of its side chapels, its restored six-storied steeple, probably to some extent the exact copy of the original one, greatly damaged in 1666 by the collapse of its spire. This steeple, second of the famous "Three Spires" is 230 feet high, while the length of the church is 194 feet, the chancel being longer than the nave. In spite of exterior recasing, poorly-restored window tracery, and some modern interior decoration, the architectural dignity and the beauty of the church make a big impression on the beholder....

...Among the church's unusual features is the stone pulpit (about 1470) richly decorated, with sides of open panel work, attached to the south-west tower pier. The brass eagle lectern with little lions at the foot is of the same date...

...The registers contain entries of a Coventry family of Shakespeares in the sixteenth-seventeenth centuries, and also one of the burial of Bartholomew Griffin (1602), an Elizabethan sonnet writer. A transatlantic interest lies in the record (April 9th 1597) of the baptism of John Davenport, who in 1637 emigrated to America, and, with Theophilus Eaton, another Coventry worthy, founded Newhaven, Connecticut. In this church, the great actress, Mrs Siddons (Sarah Kemble) was married on November 25th, 1773.

"THE ARCHITECTURAL DIGNITY AND BEAUTY OF THE CHURCH MAKE A BIG IMPRESSION ON THE BEHOLDER." So said Mary Dormer Harris of Holy Trinity Church in Coventry. The ancient brass lectern can be seen to the left and the unusual stone pulpit, erected around 1470, is on the right.

North of Trinity Church, and occupying the slope towards the Sherbourne, lay the ancient Cathedral of St Mary, and the cloisters and building of the Benedictine house, founded by Leofric and Godiva in 1043. The cathedral church, which had a thirteenth-century nave, and (probably) a Norman choir, was 600 ft long, longer than the united length of the churches of Trinity and St Michael....

...EXCAVATIONS - Excavations have revealed remains of the interior of the west-end wall, bases of piers (responds), and steps of a newel staircase in the south-west tower, which can be seen from the path between the Girls' School and the graveyard. The plinth of the tower on the north-west, now the basement of a dwelling house, is visible in a yard entered from New Buildings at the bottom of Butcher Row. What the church was like in all its glory, when priests chanted requiems in its chapels commemorating Bishop Pucelle, Bishop Burghill, and many others, when pilgrims flocked to the shrine of St Osburg, the local saint, we can only guess. The view of its towers (or spires) combined with the steeples of the neighbouring churches, must have been a wonderful sight....

...Of the conventual buildings, the cloisters, the chapter house, where Parliament met in 1404 and 1459, the refectory and infirmary, the treasure-house,

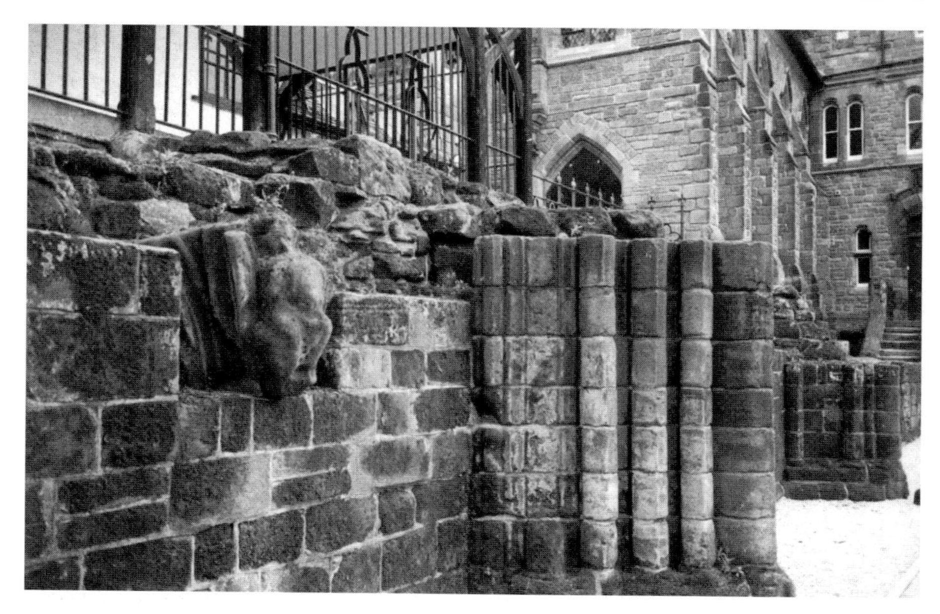

ON VARIOUS OCCASIONS MARY DORMER HARRIS DESCRIBED THE RUINS OF THE ANCIENT CATHEDRAL ADJACENT TO HOLY TRINITY CHURCH. How delighted she would have been by the recent fascinating excavations and the formation of an open area, plus a visitors' centre. This recent photograph shows the bases of the pillars which were uncovered in Victorian times.

the muniment chamber, the herbary chamber, the "seyn" chamber, where the monks were let blood at certain times of the year, not a trace now remains above the ground....The bishop of the diocese had no need to lodge at the monastic house, since the monks granted him land whereupon to build a palace in Henry III's reign. The remains of this episcopal dwelling to the north-east of St Michael's were cleared away at the building of the modern Priory Street.

ST JOHN'S CHURCH AND THE BABLAKE BUILDINGS - Facing the wayfarer at the dip at Smithford Street end is the Church of St John the Baptist, anciently served by a college of priests maintained by the Trinity Guild...

...On entering the church, the loftiness and fine proportions of the arcading strike the beholder...

BOND'S HOSPITAL - The gabled house is a reconstruction made in 1832 of the former hospital. Some of the ancient timbers, however, found their place in the new building. A beam in the east gable shows a carving of an angel and a shield of the Five Wounds....

...In the garden of this delightful place is a fragment of the old Town Wall, now scheduled as an Ancient Monument under the care of the National Trust.

A RECENT PHOTOGRAPH OF A DELIGHTFUL CORNER OF OLD COVENTRY WHICH HAS CHANGED LITTLE SINCE THE EARLY TWENTIETH CENTURY. Bond's Hospital is on the left and the former Bablake School on the right.

BABLAKE SCHOOL - On the east side of the court is the old Bablake School, which until the new building at Coundon was opened in 1890, served generations of Coventry boys for more than three hundred years. It is a half-timber dwelling of the sixteenth century...

...On the ground floor of the house is a delightful ambulatory, and the passage on the upper floor, open to the air, makes a "double cloister" such as appears in the Prior's House at Much Wenlock. From the entrance of the school a passage leads to the central hall or kitchen, open to the roof. Massive timbers, a great central chimney, and a Charles II staircase, which with its galleries occupies three sides of the room, all go to make up a delightful interior. The old refectory adjoining contains the boys' remarkable trestle table, with burr-elm top (as a great authority on furniture says) also a Jacobean mantlepiece with arcading and plain shields, dated 1629, relic of a house long since demolished, where Sir Orlando Bridgeman lived in Little Park Street. This room and those on the upper floor are devoted to the City Museum, and in them are housed relics from prehistoric to modern times, connected with Coventry history or product of excavations in the country round.

ST JOHN'S HOSPITAL, PALACE YARD AND OTHER PLACES - From Whitefriars, those who desire to make the large circuit of Coventry sights should take the Gulson Road, and seek, at the end of Far Gosford Street, the historic Gosford Green, where on September 17th 1397, Richard II stayed the proposed duel between Henry Bolingbroke and Mowbray, Duke of Norfolk, as all readers of Shakespeare's play know well. Other historical happenings have left memories about this patch of greensward, since here, in 1467 Earl Rivers and John Woodville, father and brother of the Queen of Edward IV, were beheaded by order of Warwick, the King-maker. In Gosford Street, we are reminded of the ancient representations on movable stages or "pageants" by the Coventry craft-guilds, of scenes from Biblical and legendary history, performances witnessed in their heyday by Margaret of Anjou, Richard III and Henry VII. The acting of these Mystery Plays at the feast of Corpus Christi only ceased in 1580, after they had brought crowds to the city yearly for probably close on two centuries. Gosford Street was the scene of the first performance in the morning of the feast, and the pageant-houses, where the guilds stored their stages and properties were, in many cases, situated in this neighbourhood...

IN 1935 MARY DORMER HARRIS WROTE ENTHUSIASTICALLY ABOUT THE COOK STREET GATE IN COVENTRY. This contemporary photograph was taken by her friend Philip Chatwin.

THE CITY WALL - North and north-east of Gosford Street, by way of Cox Street, Ford and Hales Streets, can best be seen the remains of the ancient city wall, begun in 1356, and all but destroyed in 1662, a mural circuit of two and a quarter miles, of great breadth, built of ashlar on the outside, with a core of rubble stones and mortar, and strengthened by thirty-two towers. Entry was afforded by twelve gates. Thus Coventry was the most considerable fortified area in the Midlands, and Richard II helped in work of building by a grant of stone from his quarry at Cheylesmore. At the back of Godiva Street, and alongside a pathway reached by steps in Hales Street, are noteworthy relics of these immense fortifications, and close to the Hales Street fragment stands the postern-gate of Swanswell, now converted into a dwelling with gabled roof. The archway is blocked up, but a little trefoil-headed double window in the top story remains. More striking is the Cook Street Gate, still further north in an insalubrious quarter that will, no doubt, soon disappear. The gate may be reached by St Agnes' Lane. This is a mere roofless shell, but at least the archway is open; and this recent gift to the city has been, of late, well preserved and restored. All the other gates are gone.

At the corner of Hales Street stands the old Grammar School, anciently the church of the Hospital of St John the Baptist, a building mainly of the early fourteenth century, but curtailed at its western end...

PALACE YARD - Coventry was famous for its fine old houses, and as the wayfarer returns from Hales Street up the main thoroughfares of Cross Cheaping and High Street, he may observe that modern building has not, as yet, quite ousted the gracious outlines of an earlier day. Happily Palace Yard, in Earl Street, has been saved from the destroyer...

....Recent repairs have converted finely-timbered chambers into committee rooms for church purposes. The whole scheme of restoration is a notable example of what might be done to preserve historic dwellings from decay and destruction.

FORD'S HOSPITAL, GEORGE ELIOT'S HOME AND OTHER PLACES - To the south of High Street, in Grey Friars Lane, stands the best preserved of all Coventry's treasures of domestic architecture, the women's alms-house, Ford's Hospital. This wonderful bit of Tudor building owes its origin to the piety and charity of William Ford, merchant of the Staple (1509) and of William Pisford (1517) and the foundation document (1529) convenants for the maintenance by the charity of "six poor men and their wives being of the age of threescore years or above, and such as were of good name and fame..." Happily the charity survived the suppression of the guild at the Reformation. It is now only aged women who profit by the worthy merchant's benevolence.

FORD'S HOSPITAL - The timber-built frontage of the hospital, with its three gables and overhanging upper story rests on a basement of stone...

...GEORGE ELIOT AND COVENTRY - ...The novelist's familiarity with Coventry suggested, no doubt, the provincial town atmosphere of "Middlemarch." She lived with her father from 1841 until 1849, at Bird Grove, at the corner of the

THE EXTERIOR OF FORD'S HOSPITAL, COVENTRY, FROM AN EARLY TWENTIETH CENTURY POSTCARD. From childhood Mary Dormer Harris would have been familiar with this building in Greyfriar's Lane, for a relation of hers, Miss Susannah Moggs, lived nearby in the Quadrant in the 1870s.

A LATE NINETEENTH CENTURY VIEW OF THE COURTYARD OF FORD'S HOSPITAL FROM AN OLD POST-CARD. Three of the women resident there (plus one man) appeared to enjoy posing for the camera.

Foleshill and George Eliot Roads, but this house, as well as "Rosehill" and "Ivy Cottage," the homes of her life-long friends, the Brays, in St Nicholas Street, lie some distance away in the north part of the city. In the Gulson Library in Trinity churchyard there is a memorial window to the novelist, and one bay of the building is devoted to the housing of editions of her works, letters, and other relics, including the statuette copy of Thorswaldsen's "Christ" which she kept before her when writing the translation of Strauss's "Life of Jesus" at Bird Grove.

To the artist, architect, and leisurely tourist, a stroll about the older streets of the city cannot fail to bring its delights...At the corner of Pepper Lane and High Street is a fine early Tudor house with overhanging stories; another charming example of the timbered house with carved corner posts stands opposite the south west door of St Michael's.

ROUGH CAST BUILDINGS - Other houses of a slightly later date have their timbers coated with rough cast...Priory Row, north of Trinity Churchyard, has the dignified air of a cathedral close, and the Priory Rooms, a classic house in brick and stone, fronted by vine-patterned iron gates, is a testimony to the skill and taste of some early eighteenth-century builder.

"ANOTHER CHARMING EXAMPLE OF THE TIMBERED HOUSE WITH CARVED CORNER POSTS STANDS OPPOSITE THE SOUTH-WEST DOOR OF ST MICHAEL'S." This Florence Weston drawing of Bayley Lane, Coventry, in the 1920s, not only shows the old house but the side of St Mary's Hall and the old pump.

PRIORY ROW, COVENTRY, FROM A POSTCARD DATED 1909.

Interesting details of mediaeval wood-carving appear in unexpected places...

...Nor should “Peeping Tom” be forgotten, gazing from the window at the corner of Smithford and Hertford Streets. The wooden figure, badly hacked, and crowned with an unsuitable hat, is ancient, dating, as the armour shows, from Henry VII’s time, but its history is unknown. Tradition has linked this figure with the Godiva legend, and with the name of this far-famed lady it is meet that this account of Coventry’s buildings and their history should close.

WESTWOOD AND TILE HILL

“How changed is here each spot man makes or fills!”

No poet has ever rhymed about the overgrown hamlets I write of; nevertheless, the changes fill with a foolish melancholy those who come back to them after a long lapse of years. Old ways and old men pass; youth builds and straightens; cities stretch out their long arms by waysides that once were green. I suppose that more people enjoy the country than they did when I was young; only the country itself has become less beautiful.

CHANGES - At Canley, one misses at once the ford where our old grey horse used to stop and drink. The little stone bridge is ship-shape of course; convenient, too; only you will forgive me for saying I liked better the old wooden footbridge and the sight of the running stream. You see, I was familiar with it all many years ago. Canley is transmogrified, too, evidently in train for a new suburb, the lanes indicated by miniature sign posts waiting to be turned into real streets. There are villas in the lane towards the Fletchamstead gate, and allotments with yellow flowering cabbages come up close to the house itself.

FLETCHAMPSTEAD - I had no right to go up to the old house. Please do not tell those in authority that I went along the grass-grown ways, and into the little gate under the immense dark yew. It was all very still save for the riot of birds in the neglected garden. I think I knew I should find no one; and, indeed, no one answered, though I waited at the door. It was foolish, because I wanted no stranger's greeting - and no greeting comes from the dead! But there was no one in the house but the "listeners": "the phantom listeners" (you know Walter de la Mare's poem). It rang in my head then; it has rung there since.

"Tell them I came, and no one answered,
I have kept my word, he said."

You know how it is when a house is quite empty, and yet you feel, you feel...

Peeping in at the curtainless window, I saw the bare room, where my cousin's harp used to to stand, and in at the one on the other side of the door , where my uncle used to read his prayers after breakfast in his dear, husky voice, and a "chapter"- from Galatians, perhaps - every morning. In the evening, when the lamp was lit, and the womenfolk had brought out their sewing, he would also read aloud from some improving book. I remember one was the biography of Frank Buckland, the naturalist. I liked better a tale in which the animals themselves talked, as they do in "The Water Babies," which was also one of my uncle's favourites.

JAMES HARRIS - Even now I associate his memory with the scent of flowers. He would gather jasmine for you from the tree which grew up by the side of the door. Evening-scented stock was sown in the garden; and year by year the evening primrose came up; and - as I live by bread! - there are leaves of evening primrose coming up among the wild growth of the garden now, amid forget-me -not and clumps of blue and white hyacinth, looking like a piece of heaven's sky fallen to the ground.

I have written before of my uncle, James Harris, who passed his whole life here, of his gentleness, his love for children, the mild radiancy of his cherubic face which no sorrow could dim, of his everlasting goodness to men and animals whose working lives were well-nigh done. Now I seem to see that Fate, which dealt so hardly with him in all appearance, giving him neither wife nor child, and taking away wealth and health - almost all he had - was really kind. For nothing harmed his soul, or robbed him of his serenity, his sweetness, the mild uncomplaining patience with which he bore all things, until there was bestowed on him the last great gift of a swift and painless death. As for his memory, it is like a beatitude -

"The actions of the just
Smell sweet and blossom in the dust."

You may live clothed in purple and fine linen, and leave a million behind you; there are no pockets in a shroud! Your name may resound through the five continents of the known world. Yet this may be lacking to you: the memory that fills the souls of those that knew you, with a perfume like that of blossoming flowers.

12. THREE NEWSPAPER ARTICLES

In the course of her life Mary Dormer Harris wrote numerous articles for newspapers and magazines. There follows three of of these articles which have not been re-published in book form.

Although the text of the Stoneleigh Mummers' Play was published in "Notes and Queries", in January 1925, the undated article re-printed here has an additional paragraph. It was probably first printed in a Midlands newspaper one Christmas in the 1920s and the text is taken from a cutting now in the collection of the Mary Dormer Harris Memorial Bursary Trust.

Unlike many other academic historians of her time, Mary Dormer Harris had much time for old legends and customs for she recognised that in the unsophisticated stories lay a great deal of social history and clues to the lives led by the ordinary people. In a long essay "Historic Warwickshire" contained in the book "Memorials of Old Warwickshire" (ed Dryden; Bemrose and Son, 1908) she declared,

"...it is not only priggish, it is unscientific, to despise legends, so valuable is the kernel they often contain, the memory of the customs, magic, fear, or ritual of a primitive people."

It was no doubt this spirit which led her to write down the words of the old Stoneleigh Mummers' Play.

1) THE CHRISTMAS MUMMERS OF STONELEIGH
by Mary Dormer Harris

This I took from the lips of one who played the Doctor's part long ago. There are seven characters in the piece. The Forman has a traditional broom to sweep a place for his actors.

"King George" and "Bold Slasher" wear red coats, silver braided caps and carry wooden swords. The Doctor has a top-hat, frock coat, white front and kid gloves. "Tom Fool" wears a white hat and is dressed in patchwork for motley. "Moll Finny" has women's clothes, bonnet and umbrella. "Humpty Jack" wears an old dented box hat, carries a stick and on his back a bag of straw. The last three have their faces blackened.

(Forman knocks at the door)

For. Would you like to pass a time with the Mummers?
Good Master and Mistress, I hope you are within,

I've come this merry Christmas time to see you and your kin.
I hope you won't be angry, nor take it as offence
For if you do, pray tell to me, and we'll quickly go from hence.
A. E. I. O. U. Downderry:
We come this merry Christmas time for to be merry.
Activity of youth, activity of age,
Activity you never saw before on a common stage.
A room, a room, to let us in,
We're none of your ragged sort, but some of your best of kin.
If you don't believe what I do say,
Step in King George and clear the way.
(The Forman is now inside the house. Enter King George)

K.G. I am King George, this noble knight.
I shed my blood for England's right,
For England's right and England's reign.
For over it I will maintain.
(knock at the door)
Hark, hark, I hear somone knock.
Pray who art thou that is knocking?
(enter Bold Slasher)

B.S. I am a valiant soldier bold,
Bold Slasher is my name.
From those cruel wars I came.
And, pray, who art thou?

K.G. I am King George, this noble knight.
I shed my blood for England's right,
For England's right and England's reign,
And England's glory I'll maintain.

B.S. A battle, a battle, betwixt you and I,
To see which of us first shall die.
So guard thy head, defend thy blows,
Likewise take care of face and nose.
(They fight. King George falls.)

For. Doctor, Doctor, do thy part.
King George is wounded through the heart;
Likewise ten times through the knee.
Five hundred pounds to cure thee.
Doctor, Doctor, don't delay,
But spur thy horse and come this way.
(Enter Doctor, riding on Tom Fool's back. Fool goes out.)

D. Here I are, the seventeenth son of a well-known doctor.
I travel here, I travel there.

	I travel at home, I come from home. I ain't one of those quick-quack, three fardin' doctors. I go about for the good of the world, not to kill but to cure.
For.	What can you cure Doctor?
D.	I can cure all sorts of complaints and diseases. Just whichever me and my box of pills pleases, *(holds up pill-box)* Such as soft corns, hard corns, molly-grubs, solly-grubs, And all such tinklehairy things as these, The itch, the stitch, the stone, the palsy and the gout, Pains within and pains without.
For.	Well, Doctor, is that all you can cure? Can you tell me how to cure the magpie of the toothache?
D.	Yes, I can
For.	How should you cure him?
D.	I should cut his head off and throw his body in the ditch. It is a sure cure, and he's out of the way. If any old man or old woman can do more than this, let them step in and try. *(enter Moll Finny)*
Moll.	Who do you call Moll Finny? My name's not Moll Finny. My name is Mrs Finny. A woman of great pain (sic) can cure more than you, or any other man again.
D.	Pray, what can you cure, Moll?
Moll.	I can cure this man if he ain't quite dead. *(goes to King George's feet)* Come now, young feller, rise up thy head.
D.	That's the wrong end, Moll.
Moll.	That's my beef-steak for once. *(goes to his head)*
D.	What's the matter with him, Moll?
Moll.	He's got the gout.
D.	What's a good thing for the gout, Moll?
Moll.	Draw a tooth.
D.	Come out of my road. Seven years' apprenticeship and seven years' journey-man ought to know better than you. Fetch my barnacles.
Moll.	Fetch 'em yourself.
D.	Fetch my pliers. *(Moll goes out for pliers and brings them back broken.)*
D.	Now you've brought 'em, you've broke 'em. Where did you break them?
Moll.	Over the tumbledown stile where the dead donkey kicked the blind man's eye out.
D.	That's a funny place, Moll.

Moll. Yes, up Blue-jacket Lane

D. *(having extracted a huge tooth, presumably from the patient's mouth)*
It's as long as a wet week.
(King George rises. Enter Humpty (or Humpy) Jack.
Tom Fool, bearing a tamburine follows)

Hum. Here come I, old Humpty Jack,
With my wife and family at my back,
Some at the workhouse, and some at my back,
And I'll bring you the rest when I come back.
In comes I, that's never been yet,
With my big head and little wit.
My head so big and my wits so small,
So I brought my music to please you all.
(plays mouth organ)
My father drunk all the tea; my mother gave me the tea-pot to make a hurdy gurdy on.

* Come lads and lasses, come fill up your glasses,
And give us poor lads some beer.
(I am not sure who says this)*

In spite of superfluous "gag" this version of the Mummers' play, which to some extent resembles others already printed from Newbold-on-Avon and Lutterworth, has much interest for the scholar. No book that I have read quite solves the problem of the black-a-vised man-woman, Moll Finny - here the Doctor's rival - and big headed Humpty Jack. They seem, however, to belong to some ancient rite when a victim perished to ensure the fertility of the fields, while in the drama proper, the restoration of a dead, or wounded, man to life and vigour, is always symbolic of the "death" of winter and the renewal of vegetation in spring. It is all as old as the hills. In some parts of the country, the Morris or sword-dance appear rather than the drama of St George; while at Warsop in Nottinghamshire some observance prevailed, of which I would fain know more. A friend tells me that, passing through the snow-clad, moon-lit village at midnight, on Christmas Eve 1890, he saw men in black - clad in tights, he says - dancing round a fire, the women in the meantime making music with beating on pots and pans. It sounds magical and very queer, but more I know not.

The Mummers' Play of St George is a last, a degenerate, example of the art of the countryside, once the home of ballad and dance and song. Life is ebbing from the villages, as it ebbs from the hardy champion of the rustic stage. Ye kindly gods of the brown earth and flowing stream, bring we pray you some great and magic healer to restore to the perishing life of the countryside the old time vigour and joy. Light the fire on the village hearth again so that there may be a "merrie Christmas" in "merrie England" once more.

THE STONELEIGH MUMMERS' PLAY WAS FIRST COLLECTED BY MARY DORMER HARRIS IN 1925. The play was revived by the Coventry Mummers in 1975 and it has been performed in Stoneleigh on Boxing Day every year since then. In this photograph, taken at Christmas 1998, in the back row (left to right) are Bryan Bellingham as Moll Finney, Jim Brannigan as King George, Gary Wilkinson as the Doctor, Graham Hall as Big Head and Dick Dixon as Humpty Jack. In the front row are Mick Barwell as Bold Slasher and Tim Chatham as the Foreman. Murray Chatham (right) is a young supporter.

****

NOTE - In an old envelope in the box of memorabilia collected by the Trustees of the Mary Dormer Harris Memorial Bursary over the years are three typewritten copies of the Stoneleigh Mummers' Play. A note on the coffee-stained envelope tells us that the play, collected by Mary Dormer Harris, was read at Christmas 1935 at 147 Leam Terrace (the home of Geoffery and Gertrude Bark). Taking part in the reading were Mary Dormer Harris (presumably as Forman) Geoffrey and Gertrude Bark, D. Knight, Clifford Sleath and Philip Styles.

That Christmas of 1935 was Mary Dormer Harris's last.

On June 8th 1923 the following article by Mary Dormer Harris appeared in the "Leamington Spa Courier". The cutting I used is preserved in the archives of the Mary Dormer Harris Memorial Bursary Trust.

2) CUCKOW CHURCH AND RYKMERSBERY A STUDY IN RURAL DEPOPULATION

by Mary Dormer Harris

There is a very striking fact of English history and of the English countryside. The people have left the land. Our villages, says the foreigner, are poetry itself -- only they are deserted. We turned down arable to pasture 1400-1600 and grew rich; we enclosed open fields and commons some 200 years later and fed a growing (and indifferently happy) population in the Napoleonic Wars. Towns filled and we repealed the Corn Laws, always, always, with an emptying countryside. The Empire grows, but the village population shrinks and dwindles, and the name of the hamlet is forgotten; it has disappeared from the earth.

Sometimes it is to make room for deer that the countryman's home vanishes, as in the Hampshire of William the Conqueror or the modern Highlands; sometimes it has been to make room for sheep, as in Tachbrook Mallory in the reign of Henry VII, when William Medley - you may see the memorial brass in Whitnash Church to his father, Benedict - and Ralph Abbot of Kenilworth drove forth sixty persons; sometimes it has been to save rates. For the most part the people have been silent, going forth "mournfully," "tearfully" dolorose, lacrimose, as the Latin of the Commissioner of 1517 says - but once in 1607 they found voice. Shakespeare, in 1608-9, transferred the scene to early Rome, but it is pure Warwickshire for all that. "You are all resolved to die rather than famish?" ...."What authority surfeits on would relieve us...let us revenge this with our pikes ere we become rakes; for the gods know I speak this in hunger for bread, not in thirst for vengeance," says the First Citizen in the opening act of "Coriolanus". "For better it were in such case we manfully die," said the Warwickshire "Diggers" who came with other Midlanders in their thousands to Hillmorton, "then hereafter to be pined to death for want of that which these devouring encroachers do serve their fat hogs and sheep withal"...Encroaching tyrants" they cried in the wonderful metaphorical English of the day, would "grind our flesh upon the whetstone of poverty...so that they may dwell by themselves in the midst of their herds of fat wethers." "Woe unto them" said an older writer in the time of an economic crisis in an eastern land, "that join house to house, that lay field to field ...that they may be placed alone in the midst of the earth."

There is one church and hamlet in a country of vanished hamlets and of ancient park and chase, that has so utterly disappeared that one almost doubts its existence. There is Rous' mention of it - Rous was the chantry priest of Guys-cliffe, who protested against enclosures in the 15th century - this evidence has been accepted by Dugdale. I am told, too, that ancient foundations are turned up when the ploughshare passes over Cuckow Hill, but there is nothing now but wide country there. And the name, surely, is country enough since it is called after the bird with the "wandering voice." Does the old woman open her basket on the hill to let the cuckoo out as she does - so they say in Sussex - at Heathfield Fair? Or did the foolish folk of Rykmersbury build a wall to keep in the cuckoo like the Gotham people long ago?

"Cuckow Church and Rykmersberg" (or Rykmersbery) are marked as existing formerly (olim) on the map of the Knightlow Hundred in Dugdale's "Warwickshire" and there is just one other deed, probably late 12th century, given in Ryland's "Wroxall" that mentions "Rykenylesbury" That is all the evidence I know of for its existence. Long before Dugdale's time the hamlet had disappeared; indeed, there were no inhabitants to rebuild the church when, in 1500, its site, chapel and chapelyard - with an endowment of 40s a year - was bestowed by Henry VII on the Dean and Chapter of St Mary's Warwick, to be reconverted to uses of piety. The Dean and Chapter satisfied everyone's conscience by taking the money; there has been no attempt to rebuild Cuckow Church. The site is given over to what the record Dugdale quotes would call "prophane" uses still, that is to say the plough travels across it and sheep nibble the growing corn.

Cuckow Hill stands a little west of Bannerhill farmhouse and south of the Gospel Oak, on the boundary between Warwick and Beausale. You may reach it from wide-bordered Rouncil Lane, which recalls another vanished hamlet, the "Rincile" of Domesday. Wedgnock Park stretched formerly on one side of the lane and Kenilworth Park and Chase on the other. A great elm spreading like an oak stands on the crest of Cuckow Hill; there is a pit hole near with bushes round its three sides; it is a glorious place from which to see the roll of Warwickshire meadow and woodland on a day of alternate cloud and sunlight or - which is quite in accord with the traditions of the place - the steeplechase or hunt go by. So may the Rykmersbury folk have watched my lord of Warwick at the chase 600 or 700 years ago. Over the hedge is a sour-looking ploughed field - it is stiff clay hereabouts - and the little heave on its surface near the great elm may indicate the site of Cuckow church and churchyard, given over to "prophane" uses still.

A little Norman - or early English - nave and chancel must have stood on Cuckow Hill say, towards the close of the twelfth century, when Margery de Clinton, wife of John D'Abitot, endowed it with glebe and tithe. She came of pious stock. Was not her grandfather that Hugh Fitz Richard of Hatton, who, after a miraculous transportation (fetters and all) from a paynim prison to Wroxall wood, founded there a nunnery of black nuns, portions of which building stand yet? Margery's husband confirms the gift (so the deed runs) "in pure and perpetual alms" to God and the chapel of St John the Evangelist in Beausale Park, for the perpetual sustentation of a chaplain, ministering in the same (how the future mocks the plans of piety!) all the land which is Rykenleybury various portions of land connected with the name of Martin the Miller, Adam the Parker and Simon the Clerk...with tithe of the mill, of cattle born in Beausale, or curtileges and gardens, of birds and venison taken in the park (for every beast one spatulum + shoulder) of fish taken in the pool, with tithe of pannage or payment for pigs turned out into the woods and certain rights of pasture ....an endowment represented probably by Henry VII's gift to Warwick Church of 40s at a later date.

So like many another, church and hamlet have gone. Nor have I been told that before the winter's dawn on St John the Evangelist's Day you may still hear the bell ring on Cuckow Hill and listen to "the blessed mutter of the Mass" and see the shadowy forms of Margery De Clinton and Martin and Adam and Simon at their prayers. But so it may be. There is moreover, a great dam in the stream near the ford in Rouncil Lane. Could this have been where Martin's mill was? And where was the pool with the fish? When the little church and and the people's houses fell to ruin, I know not. The land (says Dugdale) passed into the hands of the Earls of Warwick about 1270 to be after included in Wedgnock Park. Did the folk of Rykmersbury perish in the Black Death of 1340? Or did they merely come between the wind and the nobility of some hunting Earl, much as the Warwick wayfarers did centuries later when the Castle magnate stopt the crossway road under his wall that led to the old mill and the bridge?

How little human nature and action change as the centuries pass.

(I am indebted to Mr Jenkyns and Mr T.Sibree. Errors, however should be ascribed to me.)

This next article was signed MDH at the end and it probably appeared in a newspaper on or around 25th August 1935 which was the 450th anniversary of the Battle of Bosworth when Richard III was killed in battle. I have taken the text from an undated cutting lent to me by Nancy Dormer Gutch, to whom I extend my thanks.

3) RICHARD THE THIRD AND HIS ASSOCIATIONS WITH THE MIDLANDS (from a Correspondent)

Richard III, who died fighting bravely on Bosworth Field just 450 years ago, had many connections with the Midlands. At the Blue Boar, Leicester, was long preserved the bed on which he lay the night before the battle, and in its false bottom his hidden treasure of £300 was brought to light in Elizabeth's reign. In a tower at Maxstoke Castle is also shown a room wherein he slept, or maybe passed one of those wakeful, conscience-tormented nights of which his biographer, Sir Thomas More, speaks.

During his stay at Warwick Castle from August 7 to 15, 1483, he gave orders, says More, for the murder of the Princes in the Tower. Whitsuntide, 1485, he spent in Kenilworth Castle, seeing the Corpus Christi religious plays at Coventry, where the representation of Doomsday and the sight of the fires at Hell- mouth may have reminded him of his misdeeds. At Nottingham the "Castle of Care," as he called it, he made his headquarters during the summer of 1485, when he waited for news of Richmond, the avenger of the little Princes, whose murder was the turning point of Richard's reign.

THE MURDER OF THE LITTLE PRINCES FROM A NINETEENTH CENTURY ENGRAVING.

The boy king Edward V, who died when he was about twelve years and nine months old, has also connections with the Midlands. He was born on November 2, 1470, in the sanctuary at Westminster, where his mother, Queen Elizabeth Woodville, had taken refuge in a moment of Lancastrian triumph, and he entered very early on the duties of his royal position. In April, 1474, he paid a State visit to Coventry, where the citizens gave the three year old boy, who came "riding in a chair," or child's side saddle, a splendid reception. They presented him with a hundred marks, a gilt cup, and, no doubt to delight his childish eyes, "a kerchief of pleasaunce about the said cup." The conduits of the city ran wine, while at various stations in the streets actors, personating Richard II, Edward the Confessor, St George, and various Biblical characters, recited verses of welcome full of unrealised hopes for the future.

A group of children representing the Holy Innocents, whose day in the calendar was considered an evil omen, took part in the show, casting down from the Cross at Cross Cheaping cakes and flowers. The prospect was then so fair that no one could have guessed how the little Prince's fate would resemble that of the babes of Judaea, victims of Herod's sword. Those about the young heir made every effort to ingratiate him with the rulers of the city. He stood Godfather to the Mayor's child, and was made brother of the leading guilds of the city. His little baby brother, Prince Richard, the Duke of York, also stayed at Coventry later in the same year, and Queen Elizabeth Woodville, by gifts of venison and gracious letters of thanks for the citizens' devotion to her children, seems to have done her best to win the hearts of the people of the place for the heirs of the Yorkist line.

Much of Prince Edward's short life was spent at Ludlow Castle under the guardianship of his mother's brother, Earl Rivers, for Edward IV sought to give prominence to his wife's relations, though the upstart Woodvilles were unpopular with the old nobility. It was at Ludlow that Edward received the news of the sudden death of his father on April 9, 1483, and from the castle there the young King set out towards London with a retinue of two thousand men. At Stony Stratford, Rivers and Lord Richard Grey, the King's maternal half-brother, unwarily left their company to pay respects to Richard Duke of Gloucester, who, also travelling Londonwards, had reached Northampton. By Gloucester's orders they were seized and denounced as traitors to the young King, in spite of his tears and protests of his uncle's Rivers's innocence. Like all who stood in Richard of Gloucester's way, they had not long to live. When the tidings of these events were borne to the Queen, for the second time she hurried to the sanctuary at Westminster, with all the late King Edward's children, including the little Duke of York.

The swiftness of the astounding happenings of the next few weeks after Gloucester was declared Protector lose no point in their telling in Shakespeare's "Richard III." On May 19th the King was lodged in the Tower, ostensibly to await his coronation. June 15 saw the execution of Lord Hastings, loyal supporter of Edward IV's children, and the next day, Elizabeth Woodville, fearing no doubt, that force would be used if persuasion failed, yielded up the little Duke of York, who joined his brother in the Tower. After this the children were never seen abroad again.

The way was now clear for Gloucester. Edward V was deposed on the grounds of the alleged unlawfulness of his parents' marriage, so on June 25 Richard III's reign began.

According to a document recently discovered at Lille, in France, Edward V realised, after the execution of Hastings that his doom was sealed, and by daily confession and penance, prepared for death. The children, at first seen in the windows of the prison, were later removed to remoter quarters of the Tower and cut off from their attendents. Immediately the rumour spread that they had been murdered; though, according to Sir Thomas More, it was not until August that two hirelings, acting under orders from Sir James Tyrell, did Richard's dreadful work. Of those concerned with the murder, Miles Forrest, one of the gaolers, died not long after in sanctuary: Dighton and his master Tyrell survived some years. Tyrell was condemned in 1502 on a charge of treason against Henry VII, wholly unconnected with these events. He probably made a confession of the Princes's murder to ease his conscience before death.

The tradition that the boys were buried under a stairfoot gained some confirmation from the discovery under a stair in the White Tower in 1674 of children's bones, which were placed in an urn in Westminster Abbey by order of Charles II. Richard's fascination is felt, however, to this day, and since Horace Walpole published in 1768 his "Historic Doubts," there have not been wanting sceptics who exonerated the children's uncle and laid the guilt of their death on the shoulders of his successor Henry VII. In order to ascertain the truth, as a matter of history, the urn was opened in the presence of the Dean of Westminster and others on July 6th 1933, and after being scientifically examined and photographed the bones were replaced a few days later. From anatomical details they were pronounced to be those of children about the same age of the young princes in 1483, not of older boys, as would have been the case had they died two years later under Henry VII. Resemblances in the skulls indicated family relationship, and the tradition of smothering received some confirmation from the fact that Edward's facial bones were stained with a substance that was probably blood. The evidence thus brought to light pointed to the guilt of the traditional murderer.

13. ARMORIAL BEARINGS OF THE CITY OF COVENTRY

Whilst every book written by Mary Dormer Harris has long been out of print, there is one explanation which she wrote which has been in print more or less constantly since the 1930s. It is currently available on a free leaflet in Coventry and is also on the City of Coventry website. The wording, as reproduced here, is taken from the leaflet, by kind permission of Coventry City Council.

THE HISTORY OF THE COAT OF ARMS

Mary Dormer Harris, the local historian thought that the elephant had a religious symbolism. The ancient 'Bestiaries' works of unnatural history, treat animals as religious types, and it is from these works that many of the animals and birds in church architecture derive.

The elephant is seen, not only as a beast so strong that he can carry a tower - Coventry's castle - full of armed men, but also as a symbol of Christ's redemption of the human race. The animal, according to one of the 'Bestiary' stories, is supposed to sleep standing, leaning against a tree. Hunters sever the trunk, and he falls helpless to the ground, until a small elephant approaches and pulls him up with his trunk.

ARMS OF CITY OF COVENTRY

THE COVENTRY COAT OF ARMS AS DEPICTED IN A DRAWING BY ALBERT CHANLER IN 1911.

Mary Dormer Harris says that "those familiar with the curious cast of mediaeval thought will not be astonished that in this story was seen a type of the fall of Adam and Eve and of Christ's redemption of the human race." The foe of the elephant was the dragon, who devoured newly-born elephants, the tempter for the foe. They eat of the forbidden fruit and are lost. They are redeemed by Christ, as also the young elephant, 'through a tree' succours those who have fallen.

The elephant then, is a dragon slayer and is associated with a tree. There is a now forgotten legend of dragon-slaying in the neighbourhood - Coventry is said to be the birthplace of St George, who slew the dragon. In the early seals of Coventry, from which the coat-of-arms derives, are shown, on one side, the combat between another dragon slayer, the Archangel Michael, and the dragon. On the other side is the elephant and castle.

Mary Dormer Harris points out that the tree has been dropped out of the armorial bearings of the city, and it is a tree from which Coventry almost certainly took its name - Cofa's tree. In the mediaeval mind, the elephant suggested the eating of the fruit of the tree of knowledge of good and evil and did not merely symbolise strength.

A RARE PHOTOGRAPH OF MARY DORMER HARRIS IN HER SITTING ROOM, TOWARDS THE END OF HER LIFE. Part of the round table, on which she completed much of her writing, is visible. It is cluttered with papers as usual.

"The history of Warwickshire is a great story in little room, one of mighty happenings in one small nook of the earth. When it has been studied more scientifically than hitherto, in Dugdale's spirit but with modern lights, we may find a great deal that may help us with modern problems. For when all is said and done, our forefathers were very little removed in feeling and thought from us, the present inhabitants of this insignificant planet."

The closing words of "Historic Warwickshire" by Mary Dormer Harris. Published in "Memorials of Old Warwickshire" 1908.

APPENDIX 1

THE MAIN PUBLICATIONS OF MARY DORMER HARRIS

* 1898	LIFE IN AN OLD ENGLISH TOWN A History of Coventry from the Earliest Times Compiled from Official Records. (378 pp. Illustrated. Published by Swan Sonnenschein & Co)
1906?	Descriptive notes to the volume "Sketches of Old Coventry" by Dr Nathaniel Troughton. (undated)
* 1908	The "SOCIAL AND ECONOMIC HISTORY" Section of the Victoria County History. Volume Two, pages 137 -182.
1908	Chapters on HISTORIC WARWICKSHIRE and THE MANUSCRIPT TREASURES OF COVENTRY in "Memorials of Old Warwickshire" edited by Alice Dryden. Pages 1-17 and 157 -168
* 1907-13	The COVENTRY LEET BOOK or Mayor's Register. 1420-1555 (Published in four parts for the Early English Text Society by Kegan Paul, Trench, Trubner & Co)
* 1911	THE STORY OF COVENTRY. Mediaeval Towns series. (345pp. Published by J.M.Dent & Sons. Illustrations by A.Chanler)
1920	UNPUBLISHED DOCUMENTS RELATING TO TOWN LIFE IN COVENTRY (Published in Aberdeen by the University Press from the Transactions of the Royal Historical Society 4th Series, Vol III)
* 1921	A SOCIAL AND INDUSTRIAL HISTORY OF ENGLAND BEFORE THE INDUSTRIAL REVOLUTION. (227pp. Illustrated. Published by Collins Clear-Type Press)
1924	THE ANCIENT RECORDS OF COVENTRY. (Dugdale Society Occasional Papers No. 1)
* 1924	UNKNOWN WARWICKSHIRE. Illustrated by J.E. Duggins. 226pp (Published by John Lane The Bodley Head: London)
1926	HISTORY OF THE DRAPERS' COMPANY OF COVENTRY. 40pp
* 1935	THE REGISTER OF THE GUILD OF HOLY TRINITY, ST MARY, JOHN THE BAPTIST AND ST KATHERINE OF COVENTRY. Transcribed and edited from the original manuscript. (published by the Dugdale Society Vol 13) see also Dugdale Society Vol 19 1944
* 1937	SOME MANORS, CHURCHES AND VILLAGES OF WARWICKSHIRE with an account of Several Old Buildings of Coventry (published posthumously by Coventry City Guild from articles which originally appeared in the "Coventry Herald." between July 1930 and February 1936.)
* 1938?	PLAYS AND ESSAYS by Mary Dormer Harris Edited by Florence Hayllar. (Published posthumously and printed by the Courier Press, Bedford Street, Leamington Spa.undated)

(* denotes a major work)

These were the main publications but there were many other articles in a variety of magazines and newspapers.

APPENDIX 2

MEMORIAL BURSARY TRUSTEES 1938 - 2001

1938 -1964 Philip Chatwin Chairman 1938 -1964 (d. 1964)
1938 -1990 Gertrude Bark Secretary 1938 -1984 (d. 1990)
1938 -1952 Phyllis Hicks Joint Secretary 1938 -1952 (d. 1952)
1938 -1971 Herbert M. Jenkins Treasurer 1938 -1971. Moved.
1938 -1948 Miss E.M. Bell. Resigned 1948
1938 -1978 Miss K.S. Hill (later Mrs G. Flower). Moved (d 1978)
1938 -1944 Miss E.H.Vincent Resigned 1944
1938 -1947 Mrs Mitchell Smith (d. 1948) Coventry City Guild
1938 -1953 Mr J. Taylor (d. 1953) W.E.A.
1938 -1987 Clifford Sleath. Treasurer 1977 -1987 (d 1993)

Later co-options

1939 -1940 Rev. Ronald G. Slater (d. 1989)
1941 -1987 Miss Nora Slater. Sister of Rev. R.G. (d. 2000)
1944 -1976 Philip Styles. Chairman 1965-76 (d 1976)
1952 -1956 W.H. Perkins. Retired County Dir. of Educ.
1965 -1968 Cecily Chatwin, widow of Philip. (d 1968)
1957 -1961 Madge Lane (d. 1961) Member of Lit Soc.
1957 -1986 H.Richard Hosking. Cov College of Art. (d 1991)
1968 -1995 Robin Chapman. Tr 1971-1977. Chairman 1977-91 (d 1996)
1968 -1979 Douglas Ford. Loft Theatre. (d 1979)
1968 - *** Caroline Haynes. Sec. 1985 - 97, previously Joint Sec.
1968 -1996 Mrs Mary Elliott. Sister of Phyllis Hicks. Resigned 1996
1978 -1992 Rev. Reg. Osborn (d. 1994)
1979 -1997 Dr Rosemary Davies. Resigned 1997.
1984 - *** Angela Cameron. Chairman 1991-1999.
1984 - *** Fred Farrell
1988 - *** Syd Creed, Treasurer 1988 -***
1988 - *** John Jenkins
1991 - *** David Biddle
1994 - *** Graham Cooper. Secretary 1997 -***
1997 - *** Shirley Reading. Chairman 2000 -***
1997 - *** Jim Skinner
1998 - *** Jean Field

APPENDIX 3

BURSARY AND GRANT WINNERS 1939 - 2001

The Mary Dormer Harris Memorial Bursary was formed by public subscription in 1938. The first awards were made in 1939 and there have been eighty nine recipients since that time Over the years the amounts awarded have varied from £5 to £200 according to how much money was available and how many awards were made, but each year at least one award has been made to an able and deserving student intending to embark on higher education. It should be borne in mind that the Trustees do not have an equal number of applications each year and that some head teachers of local secondary schools rarely send in an application.

1939	James Henry Akerman of Warwick School
	Margaret Shewood of King's High School for Girls, Warwick
1940	D.A. Perrott of Warwick School
1941	Harold Austin Hill of Leamington College for Boys
1942	R.G. Bark of Warwick School
	Sheila Crouch of Leamington High School
1943	A.E.Mason of Warwick School
1944	Janet Linch of King's High School for Girls, Warwick
	Ursula Ewins of Leamington High Shool
1945	Hazel Rees of King's High School for Girls, Warwick
	June Kirby of Leamington High School
1946	Amy E. Crank of Leamington High School
1947	Frances M. Rogers of King's High School for Girls, Warwick
1948	Norman C.Simpson of the Leamington College for Boys
	June Shore, ex Leamington High School
1949	Muriel E. Smith of King's High School for Girls, Warwick
1950	D.G. Mellings of Warwick School
1951	Margaret Hughes of Leamington College for Girls
1952	Jennifer Gibbon of King's High School for Girls, Warwick
1953	J.E. Roberts, ex Leamington College for Boys
1954	Ruth Standing of Kingsley School (formerly Leamington H.S.)
1955	Maurice Henry Varney of Leamington College for Boys
	Joyce Dean of Leamington College for Girls
1956	Robin Patrick Taylor of Warwick School
1957	Alan Thomas Searle of Mid-Warwickshire School of Art
1958	Anne Caswell of King's High School for Girls, Warwick
1959	Rosemary Paget of King's High School for Girls, Warwick
1960	Caroline Haynes of Kingsley School, Leamington Spa
1961	Valerie Ley of King's High School for Girls, Warwick
1962	Marilyn Allum of Leamington College for Girls
1963	Roy D. Hogarth of Warwick School
	Vivienne King of King's High School for Girls, Warwick
1964	Rita Margaret Willis of Leamington College for Girls
1965	Lynne Warden of King's High School for Girls, Warwick
1966	Barbara Isobel Johnson of Kenilworth Grammar School
1967	James Richard Benfield of Leamington College for Boys
1968	Alison Worsley of Kingsley School, Leamington Spa

1969	Terence J. Coulthard of Leamington College for Boys
1970	Dawn C. Webber of Leamington College for Girls
1971	I.S. A. Rowlands of Warwick School
1972	Rosemary Sheppard of Leamington College for Girls
1973	Babinder Kaur Sandhar of Leamington College for Girls
1974	Elaine Valerie Edmunds of Leamington College for Girls
	Richard David Burt of King Edward VI School, Stratford
1975	Philip G. Ainsworth of King Edward VI School, Stratford
1976	David Michael Jeremy of Kenilworth Grammar School
1977	Anthony Richard Rowe of Leamington College for Boys
1978	Perry Bayliss of King Edward VI School, Stratford
1979	Amanda Ibbetson of Stratford Grammar School for Girls
1980	Caroline Murphy of King's High School For Girls, Warwick
1981	Richard Bush of Binswood Hall, North Leamington School
1982	Susan Harris of Aylesford School, Warwick
1983	Stephanie Lewis of King's High School for Girls, Warwick
1984	Sean Webb of Princethorpe College
1985	Marie Daly of Trinity School, Leamington Spa
1986	Amy Partridge of Trinity School, Leamington Spa
	Jennifer Strong of Stratford Grammar School for Girls
1987	Susan Ward of King's High School for Girls,Warwick
	Suhkjivan Hayer of Campion School, Leamington Spa
1988	Rebecca Harding of King's High School for Girls, Warwick
1989	Mark Brown of Southam School
	Gillian Harris of King's High School for Girls, Warwick
1990	Joanne Hawkins of Aylesford School,Warwick
	Dylan Kay of King Edward VI School, Stratford
1991	Stephen Ballinger of Binswood Hall, North Leamington School
	Susan Rees of Aylesford School, Warwick
1992	Leigh Fulton of Aylesford School,Warwick
	Emma Nelson of Binswood Hall, North Leamington School
1993	Brendon Hole of Aylesford School, Warwick
	Janet Leigh of Southam School
1994	Mark Atkins of Binswood Hall, North Leamington School
	Helen Bamforth of King's High School for Girls, Warwick
1995	Stephen Edwards of King Edward VI School,Stratford
	Geoff Savage of Castle Centre, Kenilworth
1996	Jody Bowers of King Edward VI School, Stratford
	Victoria Page of King's High School for Girls, Warwick
1997	Lucy Barber of Aylesford School,Warwick
	William Pettigrew of Warwick School
1998	Rebecca Vick of Kineton High School
	Adam Cox of King Edward VI School, Stratford
	Shona Mclean of Stratford Grammar School for Girls
1999	Samuel Burstall of Warwick School
	Bronwyn Davidson of Kenilworth School
	Leanne Murphy of Trinity School, Leamington Spa
2000	Celia Hughes of Kineton High School
	Ruth Whiteman of King's High School for Girls, Warwick
2001	Ryan Fawley of the Mid Warwickshire College
	Felicity Boardman of Castle Centre, Kenilworth
	Benjamin Green of King Edward VI School, Stratford

BIBLIOGRAPHY

DOCUMENTS

I conducted much research in Coventry City Archives Office where I consulted mainly the Coventry City Guild Collection (ref. 313).

The Archivist and Librarian of Lady Margaret Hall in Oxford kindly gave me access to archive material concerning the early students (1879-1890).

I made extensive use of the wealth of material (notes, minute-books, photographs, leaflets, letters etc) contained in the Archives of the Mary Dormer Harris Memorial Bursary Trust.

Also consulted were the archives of the Loft Theatre, Leamington Spa, and the archives of the Leamington Literary Society, now housed in Warwickshire County Record Office.

PUBLISHED SOURCES

VICTORIA COUNTY HISTORY OF WARWICKSHIRE, in particular volumes 2 and 8
CHRONICLE OF THE WORLD, Longmans 1989
CHRONICLE OF THE TWENTIETH CENTURY, Longmans 1988
CITY COUNCIL MINUTES Bound volumes concerning the Corporation of the City of Coventry in the twentieth century.
HISTORY OF WARWICK AND ITS PEOPLE, by Thomas Kempe, 1905
THE LITERARY YEAR BOOK Edited Herbert Morrah (George Allen,1900)
PLEASANT SPOTS AROUND OXFORD by Alfred Rimmer
(Cassell Petter & Galpin, undated, 1880s?)
GLIMPSES OF THE PAST by Elizabeth Wordsworth (A.R. Mowbray & Co. Ltd. London and Oxford, 1912)
LADY MARGARET HALL A SHORT HISTORY edited Gemma Bailey (London, Oxford University Press, Humphrey Milford 1923)
THE LETTERS OF GERTRUDE BELL edited Lady Bell (Ernest Benn Ltd. London 1927)
OXFORD IN OLD PHOTOGRAPHS By Judi Caton (Sutton Publishing Ltd. 1988)
CAUGHT IN THE WEB OF WORDS by K.M. Elizabeth Murray (Yale University Press, Paperback Edition, 1995)
THE OXFORD UNIVERSITY PRESS, AN INFORMAL HISTORY by Peter Sutcliffe (Oxford University Press, 1978)

COVENTRY AT WAR by David McGrory (Sutton Publishing Ltd, 1997)
THE CITY OF COVENTRY, IMAGES FROM THE PAST by David McGrory (Jones-Sands Publishing, 1996)
ROYAL LEAMINGTON SPA, IMAGES FROM THE PAST by W.G. Gibbons (Jones-Sands Publishing, 1995)
THE SCHOOLGIRL ETHIC, THE LIFE AND WORKS OF ANGELA BRAZIL by Gillian Freeman (Allen Lane Penguin Books Ltd, London, 1976)
THE LEAMINGTON WE USED TO KNOW edited Kathleen Hanks (Leamington Literary Society, 1977)
MORE LOOKING BACK edited Kathleen Hanks (Leamington Literary Society, 1980)
A LAST LOOK BACK edited Kathleen Hanks (Leamington Literary Society, 1983)
THE LEAMINGTON LITERARY SOCIETY 1912-1992 (privately printed, 1992?)
NOISES ON AND OFF, 75 YEARS OF THE LOFT THEATRE, LEAMINGTON SPA, by Dorothy Fenner (Privately published, 1999)
MIRROR TO A MERMAID by Maurice Cheesewright (The University of Birmingham 1975)
DICTIONARY OF NATIONAL BIOGRAPHY - various volumes
THE TRANSACTIONS OF THE BIRMINGHAM ARCHAEOLOGICAL SOCIETY - various volumes
WARWICKSHIRE HISTORY, THE JOURNAL OF THE WARWICKSHIRE LOCAL HISTORY SOCIETY, various editions.

ALSO ALL THE MAJOR PUBLICATIONS OF MARY DORMER HARRIS (SEE LIST IN APPENDIX) AND VARIOUS EDITIONS OF LOCAL NEWSPAPERS INCLUDING "THE WARWICK ADVERTISER" "LEAMINGTON SPA COURIER" "COVENTRY HERALD" "MIDLAND DAILY TELEGRAPH" ETC, 1867 to 1938.

INDEX

BY THE SAME AUTHOR

A Tour of St Margaret's Church, Whitnash 1992
She Dyed About Midnight (Warwick), Brewin Books 1992
Beneath the Great Elms (Whitnash), Brewin Books 1993
Kings of Warwick, Brewin Books 1995
Acorns, Oaks and Squirrels, Warwick Preparatory School 1996
The Ash Grove (Whitnash), Sunken Bell Productions 1996
The Ilex & the Mulberry Tree, King's High School, Warwick 1997
Landor (a biography of Walter Savage Landor 1775-1864), Brewin Books 2000